Praise for LEFT OF BANG

W9-AKS-877

In an age when America's technological edge has eroded in military matters, Van Horne and Riley have written a compelling and detailed outline for continued American adaptation through improved tactical cunning. Using timeless and proven techniques that can put American troops above and beyond enemy capabilities, the tactical awareness they outline is stripped of mystery and presented in a compelling manner. Throughout history we have seen skilled warriors defeat enemies who are more numerous or less trained. At a time when we must adapt to the changing character of conflict, this is a serious book on a serious issue that can give us the edge we need.

—General James Mattis, USMC, Ret.

Left of Bang offers a crisp lesson in survival in which Van Horne and Riley affirm a compelling truth: It's better to detect sinister intentions early than respond to violent actions late. *Left of Bang* helps readers avoid the bang.

—Gavin de Becker,
bestselling author of *The Gift of Fear*

Rare is the book that is immediately practical and interesting. *Left of Bang* accomplishes this from start to finish. There is something here for everyone in the people business and we are all in the people business.

—Joe Navarro,
bestselling author of *What Every BODY is Saying*

Left of Bang is a highly important and innovative book that offers a substantial contribution to answering the challenge of Fourth Generation War (4GW). In 4GW, once "bang" has happened, the state has failed and its legitimacy is further eroded. All "first response" is too late. The state's focus must be prevention, and *Left of Bang* suggests concrete ways "bang" can be prevented.

—William S. Lind,
author of *Maneuver Warfare Handbook*

Left of Bang is born from the blood and fire lessons of Marines in combat. The learning curve is short in the fight and failure often means death. Seeing, recognizing, and acting on danger before the hammer falls is what *Left of Bang* is all about. To that end, Patrick Van Horne and Jason A. Riley have set forth lessons of human ability and conduct in conflict. These actions and concepts apply to each of us who fight the good fight against enemies who seek our destruction. Whether military, police, or citizen defender, to win the battle we must find a way to intercept the enemy and deter his plans—a tough challenge against an enemy who is often hiding in plain sight. *Left of Bang* contains answers to detection, deterrence, and ultimate victory. This is a warrior's book. Get it, read it, live it.

—Jeff Chudwin, Chief of Police Ret.,
President, Illinois Tactical Officers Association

An amazing book! Applying the lessons learned in the longest war in American history, and building on seminal works like *The Gift of Fear* and *On Combat*, this book provides a framework of knowledge that will bring military, law enforcement and individual citizens to new levels of survival mindset and performance in life-and-death situations. *Left of Bang* is an instant classic.

—Lt. Colonel Dave Grossman, U.S. Army Ret.,
author of *On Combat* and *On Killing*

LEFT

OF

BANG

**HOW THE MARINE CORPS'
COMBAT HUNTER PROGRAM
CAN SAVE YOUR LIFE**

**PATRICK VAN HORNE
AND
JASON A. RILEY**

DISCLAIMER

The views expressed in this book are those of the authors
and do not reflect the official policy or position of the
United States Marine Corps, Department of Defense,
or the U.S. Government.

LEFT

OF

BANG

PATRICK VAN HORNE
AND
JASON A. RILEY

Black Irish Entertainment LLC

NEW YORK   **LOS ANGELES**

BLACK IRISH ENTERTAINMENT LLC
ANSONIA STATION
P.O. BOX 237203
NEW YORK, NY 10023

COPYRIGHT © 2014 BY PATRICK VAN HORNE AND JASON A. RILEY

BOOK DESIGN BY DERICK TSAI, MAGNUS REX
FOREWORD BY STEVEN PRESSFIELD
EDITED BY SHAWN COYNE

ALL RIGHTS RESERVED

FIRST BLACK IRISH ENTERTAINMENT PAPERBACK EDITION JUNE 2014

FOR INFORMATION ABOUT SPECIAL DISCOUNTS OR BULK PURCHASES,
PLEASE VISIT WWW.BLACKIRISHBOOKS.COM OR
WWW.STEVENPRESSFIELD.COM

ISBN: 978-1-936891-30-6
EBOOK: 978-1-936891-18-4

PRINTED IN THE UNITED STATES OF AMERICA
2 3 4 5 6 7 8 9 10

We dedicate this book to the Marines who have lost life and limb fighting for their fellow Marines and for us at home. May this increase future Marines' understanding of human behavior, survivability, and lethality and decrease the enemy's effectiveness.

TABLE OF CONTENTS

FOREWORD

A DAY AT CAMP PENDLETON

I first met Capt. Van Horne and Maj. Riley (he was a captain then) when they took me through a one-day mini-version of the Combat Hunter Course at Camp Pendleton in southern California. After three minutes I thought, "This stuff has got to be made available to the wider public."

The Combat Hunter Course teaches Marines what their conventional training doesn't. Not only how to deal with the bad guys—but how to spot them in the first place, particularly when they look and act exactly like the good guys.

Left of Bang is not for combat warriors only. It's for you on the subway, you in a bad part of town, you with the sharks in the corporate boardroom. It's for your wife when she's home alone, or entering a dark parking structure, or walking with the kids on vacation overseas.

"Right of bang," as Van Horne and Riley explain in these pages, means *after* the bomb has gone off, *after* the shots have been fired, *after* the damage has been done.

"Left of bang" means *before* the bad stuff happens. That's where you want to be—alert, ready, prepared to respond to protect yourself and your loved ones.

I'm proud to be part of the team that is getting this material out, not just to soldiers and Marines in their training, but into the wider world that includes your family and mine.

Bang happens.
This book will teach you how to stay left of it.

Steven Pressfield
Los Angeles
2014

AKNOWLEDGMENTS

As Malcolm Gladwell skillfully demonstrates in his book *Outliers*, most success stories should be understood as a combination of mutually supporting factors, two of which are hard work and opportunity. We have both put hundreds of hours into researching this material, refining and further developing course material for the Marine Corps, and training Marines. Although we are nowhere near the ten-thousand hour mark needed to claim "expertise," our numerous deployments, experience, and research into these topics give us a unique insight into the type of behavioral analysis we are writing about. More important for both of us have been the opportunities we have been given: to become a part of the Combat Hunter program in the first place, to be able to build upon the work and successes of those who came before us, and to be able to work with tremendously professional and inspiring Marines within Mobile Training Company. Because we are building off of others' works, we must take a few moments to give credit to whom credit is due and to thank them for what they have done.

First, we wish to thank the Marines who have themselves spent hundreds of hours training Marines and developing courses: Major Dane Hanson, Major Keith Montgomery, Major Paul Chase, Gunnery Sergeant Gonzalez, Gunnery Sergeant Tollett, Staff Sergeant "Moose" Morris, Staff Sergeant Hammer, Staff Sergeant Baldino, Staff Sergeant Valdez, Staff Sergeant Jerew, Sergeant Arnett, Sergeant Guzman, Sergeant Syvrud, Sergeant Giles, Sergeant Gibson, and the numerous Marines who came before us. We apologize for anyone we've forgotten to include.

Second, we wish to thank the civilian instructors who passed the baton to us: Greg Williams and his colleagues poured several years into developing the Combat Profiling program and deserve full credit for the genesis of these concepts. While we have made these concepts our own, even disagreeing at many points, and have advanced thought in numerous ways, they deserve great credit for their hard work.

We also wish to thank those researchers and scientists who were generous enough to share their time and expertise with us as we conducted our research.

We also wish to thank Steven Pressfield and Shawn Coyne who believed in us and made the publication of this book possible. We would also like to thank Lisa and Angie for reading every word, listening to every rehearsal, and supporting us every step of the way. Without you, this book would never have been finished. We fully acknowledge that without these individuals this work would not exist.

Finally, we humbly thank the thousands of Marines who have deployed abroad, and who are currently deployed, ensuring the peace and freedoms we take for granted every day.

PREFACE

STRANGERS IN STRANGE LANDS

Imagine you are a U.S. Marine or soldier patrolling the crowded marketplace of a hostile enemy village. You are separated from the nearest squad member by about ninety feet, the distance between home plate and first base at a Major League ballpark. You are easily identifiable by your tan uniform, flak jacket, weapon, radio, and other gear.

The enemy is unidentifiable. The enemy could be anybody. The market is crowded. People are pushing and shoving. Some are bumping into other people to avoid you. Others don't move out of your way until you invade their personal space. Others, not paying attention, bump into you.

During your pre-deployment training, you were told to look out for military-age males when patrolling an urban area. But what does that mean? You've heard reports of ten-year-old children proficiently firing weapons. You've been told that the natives have been fighting for centuries and that some of the toughest warriors in the village are old men, elders, and warlords. So, military-age males include every man and boy in the village. You have also heard reports of female suicide bombers blowing themselves up in the midst of a patrol. How do you determine who is the threat?

On the best day, your patrol moves through the village without incident. On a good day, you observe a weapon or suicide vest, and you are able to react before the insurgent fires at you or your comrades or blows himself up. On a bad day, the enemy is too quick or too close for you to do anything at all.

All of your training stateside focused on what to do once something happens: A bullet is fired in your direction, an improvised explosive device (IED) explodes, or a mortar round impacts nearby. You can't help but wonder how you could get a jump on the bad guy—*before* the bang. How can you discern those who want to harm you from those who are just afraid or just going about their business before the attack? How can you defuse a threat before it happens? Is that even possible?

The Combat Hunter program has proven again and again that it is.

Marines and other members of the Armed Forces, law enforcement officers and other security personnel, and even the average person cannot wait for dangerous people to do bad things to them. Nor are contemporary environments of peril confined to foreign lands. The streets of Los Angeles, like the alleys of Kandahar, are complex and chaotic environments in which it is not always easy to tell the good guys from the bad guys.

The military, law enforcement, security personnel, and even civilians can use the principles of Combat Hunter to identify the three types of people in any public arena—the "shepherds" (good guys), "sheep" (regular guys), and "wolves in sheep's clothing" (bad guys).

It's not magic.

It's based on the universal patterns of human behavior. No matter the race, religion, nationality, sex, or age, people share a common physical language that can be learned and interpreted by anyone. The Combat Hunter program teaches us to do that.

Paradigm Shift — Jason A. Riley

I first learned about the Combat Hunter program after I had already deployed three times. The phrase commonly used to describe the change in mindset after a person completes a Combat Hunter course is "paradigmatic shift." After the course, you perceive the world differently. You no longer simply see footprints in the ground, but evidence of human activity. A set of footprints becomes the beginning of a track line. Before Combat Hunter, I was only partially aware of the meaning of human behavior. Like most people, I had certain intuitions about situations and other people, but I couldn't articulate them. After Combat Hunter, I had a language to describe the phenomena I witnessed and understood human behavior entirely differently. Nevertheless, I was disappointed that I could reflect on three deployments and identify numerous times in which Combat Hunter could have aided my Marines' and my ability to identify insurgents and IEDs and more effectively conduct counterinsurgency operations.

I am a suspicious person. By that, I mean that I am usually suspicious of anything new and popular, and I was immediately suspicious of this program. Combat Hunter wasn't the usual tactical course. I wasn't a believer, initially.

What is also a stumbling block for many people is that, once a person has learned about combat tracking and combat profiling, it doesn't seem complicated. It seems obvious. Of course, footprints have outlines, edges, shapes, etc. Of course, a person stepping on rocks will displace them or leave mud on the rocks. Of course, someone will act differently if they feel uncomfortable. Any fool can tell you that. But this is like saying, "Of course, the earth revolves around the sun." Combat Hunter is like a Copernican revolution of the mind. It seems obvious afterwards but is rarely realized on one's own. Another problem is that most people can't articulate what they see, and they can't say anything about the meaning of other people's actions. They usually don't do anything about other people's behavior. What Combat Hunter and especially combat profiling does is instill a mindset of proactiveness in an individual—with the tangible skills of observation, tracking, and profiling.

We've trained numerous people from outside of the military. When law enforcement agents go through our course, especially senior agents, they are consistently amazed that they were never taught these things before. Naturally, most of the senior agents tacitly know this stuff. They have years of practice of observing human behavior and, if pressed, could probably articulate most of this stuff in one way or another. However, these agents also say that what Combat Hunter, especially combat profiling, provides is a lifetime's worth of experience in a few weeks. It gives Marines and law enforcement agents explicit knowledge that would have taken years to learn on the job.

Now that I've been trained in the skills, have developed courses, and have trained other people, I believe that anyone who is concerned for their safety and the safety of others would do well to learn what we teach.

I Wish I Had This Before — Patrick Van Horne

I was first exposed to Combat Hunter after twice deploying to Iraq and spending another year preparing a company for its yearlong deployment to Afghanistan. As I sat through that first class, I couldn't stop myself from getting angrier and angrier as each class built upon the last. When it came to preparing Marines to identify an enemy hiding amongst a civilian population, the material taught during that first, two-week Combat Hunter course made it one of the best I had seen. The instructors were discussing topics and restructuring how we looked at the world, and I was mad that my units didn't get to learn this before we deployed. The course would have had a huge impact on the way we operated overseas, the way we patrolled, and the way we talked to local villagers. This had to change.

Spending the next two years leading a mobile training team, I began to see the underlying problem. It was one of exposure and distribution. We were only teaching about 40 Marines in a battalion of nearly a thousand but there was no way we could ever get this to every Marine heading downrange because it just isn't possible to provide classroom instruction to everyone. The course provided skills that might bring more Marines back alive from deployment, yet there weren't enough instructors or time to teach everyone. This had to change.

This book, our website,* and now my company exist to fix that very problem. No Marine or soldier should have to deploy without first learning how to find the enemy before he begins his attack. No police officer or security guard should have to go on patrol without knowing how to identify a criminal before he commits his crime. No person should have to wait until they see a gun to know that there is threat present.

Getting left of bang requires two things. The first is a mindset and mentality to actively search your area for people that don't fit in. The second is the knowledge to know what causes someone to stand out from the crowd. I hope that this book and the webpages that accompany these pages help provide you with what you need to do both.

---

*To see more about what drove the authors to write the book, watch an interview with them at www.cp-journal.com/leftofbang

PART ONE

THE WAR LAB

1. A MARINE CALLED "CHAOS"

In July 2006, at the height of the Iraqi insurgency, American service people were being killed and maimed in unprecedented numbers. In a single month, 1,666 IEDs were detonated, and another 959 were found waiting to explode.[1] In September 2006 alone, 776 Americans were wounded. In the first week of October, 300 more were hit.[2] In the lexicon of after-action analysis, these warriors were "right of bang." They were reactive, and the enemy triggered his explosive devices before our troops were aware of the danger.

To provide perspective concerning the destructive nature of an IED, consider the Bradley Fighting Vehicle. The Bradley is armored and heavily armed, designed to transport and provide suppressive fire for dismounted troops in an attack. Its main weapon is a 25mm cannon, which fires up to 200 rounds per minute (three to four bullets per second) at a maximum effective range of one and half miles. The Bradley also weighs approximately 22 tons. The Bradley is a ferociously powerful vehicle capable of bringing significant destructive force upon the enemy.

But even the Bradley is no match for an IED. In 2004, after a Bradley struck an IED in Iraq, its armored bottom plate was found more than 60 feet from the site of the explosion.[3] One simple, yet powerful IED can destroy a $3,200,000 machine in seconds. The destructive force is even greater when IEDs are strung together in what are called "daisy chains" or are combined with complex, direct-fire ambushes. If these statistics about IEDs are not startling enough, other intelligence estimates indicated that the insurgents were actively hunting soldiers on patrol.[4]

Beginning in 2005, several videos were released by an insurgent group called the Islamic Army in Iraq that depicted an enemy sniper killing American soldiers and Marines. This individual became known as the "Juba Sniper," and it is unknown how many soldiers and Marines he wounded before his capture. The figures are certainly in the double digits, perhaps even the triple digits. The effect of the videos and the targeting of troops on patrol was unnerving. The long hours of foot and vehicle patrols and standing guard made Marines and soldiers fatigued and complacent. The set patterns made their targeting easy. It was obvious to the troops on the ground that stateside training was inadequate in finding the sniper and others like him hiding in plain sight. The IEDs and the targeting of American forces by Iraqi insurgent snipers gravely threatened the entire U.S. war effort. Something had to be done.

The first response from the military establishment was to increase production and employment of better body armor and heavier armored vehicles. These steps helped, but they also made U.S. Marines and soldiers clumsier, slower and more obvious targets than before. It was a losing battle because the larger we made vehicles and the thicker we made armor, the larger and more deadly the insurgents made the IEDs. Although the addition of armor and other technologies helped protect troops from IEDs, we were only treating symptoms, not the cause.

Marine General James Mattis, callsign "Chaos," had a different idea. Mattis was the Commander of the First Marine Expeditionary Force, commanding all Marines in Iraq. While Mattis believed in the importance of integrating the technology, he also saw the limitations of what was then available. The technology, at the time, mostly provided a defensive capability, and he wanted to go on the offense. He wanted to take away the enemy's options of when and where the IED could be detonated. To make Marines more tactically cunning on the battlefiled, he believed in creating not only better technology but also better training. In Fall 2006, he requested that the Marine Corps develop a program to instill a hunter-like mindset in Marines, train Marines for increased situational awareness, proactively seek threats, and have a bias for action.[5] Mattis wanted Marines to be the predators, not the prey.

This directive from "Chaos" was the genesis of the Combat Hunter program.

2. LEFT OF BANG

The Marine Corps War-Fighting Lab went to work in early 2007 with the task of creating a program that gave Marines the ability to realize an attack was imminent. The preparation for an attack leaves behind cues a trained observer can pick up on to provide an early warning. Training Marines to make those observations was one of the goals of the program. In the lexicon of Combat Hunter, the purpose was to get Marines "left of bang."

If you were to think about an attack on a timeline, bang is in the middle. Bang is the act. Bang is the IED explosion, the sniper taking a shot, or the beginning of an ambush. Bang is what we want to prevent. Being left of bang means that a person has observed one of the pre-event indicators, one of the warning signs, that must occur earlier on the timeline for the bang to happen. In an IED attack, an insurgent would have to observe the Marine unit in the area, identify that they use the same road on their patrols, determine where on that road they would place the IED, acquire the materials, build the bomb, dig the hole, put the IED in the hole, connect the trigger, and watch to see if the attack was successful. Being left of bang means that we can identify the people doing the surveillance or emplacing the IED and prevent an attack from happening by stopping the process there. Being left of bang means not letting the insurgent carry through with the plan to kill American troops.

Being on the other end of the timeline is referred to as being "right of bang." Most of the training that military operators and law enforcement personnel receive is reactive. They learn skills and techniques that rely on someone else taking the initiative, which means waiting for the enemy or criminal to act first. Unfortunately, whoever strikes first possesses a powerful tactical advantage. When a person is right of bang, they are reacting to the action that took place. After the IED detonates, then the Marines establish security on that site. After the IED detonates, then the Marines treat their casualties. After the IED detonates, then the unit returns fire on the enemy. Whenever a person is operating right of bang, it means that the enemy has the initiative and controls the situation.

But operating left of bang requires intense concentration to identify the pre-event indicators and gain an advanced warning about the enemy's intentions. These indicators, however, are not always easy to discern. If the first time a Marine realizes a threat is present is when he sees an AK-47 assault rifle aimed in his direction, he has already lost the

initiative and is now r...
bang requires that he can ...
build an enhanced awareness ...

3. COOPER'S COLU...

In February 2013, New Orleans police on...
responded to a report of a robbery at a local L... ral
store.[6] It was about 7 a.m. The information gi... ,y the
dispatcher was vague. Going into the situation, Officer
Passaro was unsure if the store or an individual had been
robbed. He was unsure if the assailant was still at the scene
or if he had fled. He did not know if the robber was armed.
When Officer Passaro arrived at the scene, he did not see
anyone in the store. Backup was on the way, but Passaro
decided to enter the store on his own anyway. As he made
his way through the store, he noticed the door to the
manager's office was closed. He approached the door and
announced that he was a police officer. Immediately, the
robber opened the door and fired on Passaro, hitting him
twice and leaving him in critical condition. The shooter fled.
Thankfully, backup arrived within seconds of Officer
Passaro being shot, and his life was saved.

Right now, there is insufficient information to know
exactly what Passaro's actions were at the scene. It is
unknown if he had drawn his gun. Initial interviews and
reports of the incident have placed some blame on the
unclear, ambiguous information given the officer. Capt.
Michael Glasser, president of the Police Association of New
Orleans, stated, "Had there been any indicator it was in
progress, I'm sure he would've acted differently." There is
certainly some truth to this. Better information definitely
would have influenced Officer Passaro to take different
actions. If he had known that the robbery was still in

would have waited for backup. ...art III, a lawyer and spokesman for the local ...al Order of Police lodge, was adamant that, "The way ... communications relayed it to (Passaro), the officer did not have accurate information to make the proper decision." This is probably true, but certainly not the only reason events unfolded as they did.

In analyzing this situation through the lens of combat profiling, we want to raise the issue of awareness. In no way do we want to portray Officer Passaro badly, and we certainly do not have enough information to criticize his actions. Regardless of what Officer Passaro did or did not do, he is not at fault for his shooting. No one has the right to fire on a law enforcement agent, and the only one guilty in this situation is the perpetrator. Nevertheless, it is appropriate to discuss the situation to learn from it. The situation could be viewed from multiple perspectives. Tactically, perhaps Officer Passaro could have positioned himself better (at an oblique angle from the door) or ensured he had cover before announcing himself.

Our focus is the psychological perspective. What was Officer Passaro's awareness at the scene? Was he of the mindset to respond with lethal force, even if he didn't have positive information that the robbery was still in progress, or was he unprepared and unready to take lethal action?

From the perspective of combat profiling, a basic mental preparedness to take lethal action may be the difference between life and death. Retired Marine Lt. Col. Jeff Cooper developed a system of awareness he called his Color Code that described the psychological conditions a person could have during any given situation. Cooper's Color Code possesses four levels of awareness: White, Yellow, Orange, and Red.

Condition White means being unprepared and unready to take lethal action. A person who is in Condition White is in a low state of psychological awareness and physiological arousal—if attacked, this person will likely be the victim. This person believes his or her personal safety is not in jeopardy and has chosen not to actively assess the surroundings for potential threats. Should a threat arise because of a lack of awareness, that person would be completely unprepared, forcing them to be reactive.

Condition Yellow means that the person understands that his or her life is in danger and is therefore psychologically prepared to do something about it. This person is actively searching the surroundings to find a threat because he or she is in a moderate level of psychological awareness and physiological arousal. Once a person has recognized a threat, they have escalated to Condition Orange.

Condition Orange is the mindset in which a person is focused on a specific threat and is prepared to take action against that threat. This person is actually in a lower state of psychological awareness than in Condition Yellow but in a higher state of physiological arousal. This person has begun creating a plan for how to deal with the threat. The degree of awareness a Marine has here is less than that of Condition Yellow because the person's attention is now focused on a specific threat.

Condition Red is labeled the "lethal mode"—it is the psychological willingness to kill if circumstances warrant that action. Condition Red includes being "in the fight" and executing the plans created in Condition Orange. This person is in a much lower state of awareness due to being focused on one specific threat and has a very high degree of physiological arousal. Because of the inherent risk of engagement in a fight, the person's awareness of the surroundings is further reduced as his or her mental capacity is focused on personal challenges to survival. Based on research by retired Lt. Col. David Grossman and others, the Marine Corps has adapted Cooper's Color Code to describe physiological arousal and awareness levels.

In the Marine Corps' system, another color condition exists: Condition Black. Condition Black is characterized by when a person's heart rate reaches a point that is counterproductive (above 175 beats per minute) and that person begins to lose awareness of the surroundings. A person in Condition Black can no longer cognitively process information and may completely shut down.[7]

The normal psychological state of anyone concerned about personal safety must be Condition Yellow. This means being aware of one's surroundings, looking for potential threats, and being alert, no matter the situation. Combat profiling rests on the assumption that being proactive, being left of bang, requires continuous awareness and alertness. It requires that the combat profiler always be psychologically prepared to take action. From this perspective, Officer Passaro's situation can be evaluated differently. Although he may not have had accurate information about the crime in progress, that should not have mattered to him. Any police officer responding to a scene should be psychologically prepared to use deadly force, if necessary. Regardless of whether one knows danger is present, one should be ready to take action and be looking for indicators of a threat.

In the aftermath of the shooting, Capt. Michael Glasser, the Police Association of New Orleans president said, "You anticipate that back-up is coming, and you anticipate that this is probably going to be like all the other calls." From the perspective of combat profiling this is the opposite of what we want people to think. You should never anticipate "this is probably going to be like all the other calls." Marines, police officers, and anyone who wants to survive an attack must never be caught off guard. Every situation must be considered potentially dangerous, and you must be constantly ready to take action if a threat emerges.

4. RE-ENGINEERING THE TOOLKIT

Marines, soldiers, police officers, and basically anyone who operates in a complex and potentially hostile environment must make tough decisions under severe duress, usually with little time and information.

Not only must the Marine identify the enemy, but he also must consider the various rules of engagement* and escalation of force** measures—and ensure he has positive identification (PID) on the enemy before returning fire. What many do not understand is that, though these measures are supposed to facilitate decisions, to the rifleman on patrol, these measures seem constraining, hindering, and overburdening. The average Marine's head spins when trying to consider all of these factors while simultaneously keeping himself and his fellow Marines alive.

Since the invasion into Afghanistan in 2001, Marines have been put into countless bad situations, and while some have made less than ideal decisions that have gotten a great deal of attention in the media, the vast majority of Marines have made great decisions and have shown incredible insight, sharpness of mind, unerring intuition, and the ability to

---

*Rules of engagement are the circumstances that must be met for the military to employ lethal force in combat situations. Usually, they encompass, at a minimum, identifying either a hostile act or intent and having a positive identification of that person. These are customized by the Commanding Officer in different engagements and can be changed to meet the needs of that unit.

**Escalation of force measures are the conditions that must be met to elevate from a less than lethal reaction to lethal action against a perceived threat. These measures are taken to help reduce the risk of unnecessary casualties, whether military or civilian.

examine a situation and know exactly what to do. Here's the problem: It's all chance. There's no way to tell from one Marine to the next who will have the keenness of intellect to make good decisions on the battlefield and who will fail. Currently, it's not entirely based on the training they receive. A Marine's ability to make decisions is mostly due to his or her life and experiences. The Marine cannot control much of this. Some Marines can quickly identify certain patterns in Afghanistan because they have, for instance, experiences staying safe in dangerous areas of New York or L.A. They have what we call "thick file folders," a significant amount of relatable experiences they can quickly access in similar situations abroad. But certain Marines having these experiences is simply coincidental—they just happened to have grown up in a dangerous environment. Other Marines aren't so lucky and do not have the experiences needed to make the same decisions driven by intuition.

Intuition is a powerful force; however, it is poorly understood. Intuition is not black magic or some inexplicable force of nature. Intuition is nothing more than *a person's sense about a situation influenced by experience and knowledge.* Intuition is the way the mind picks up on patterns and uses experiential and learned knowledge to guide a person during a given situation. However, intuition is often driven by the subconscious. It's rightly called a "gut feeling," since people can literally have a physical response when their intuition tries to make them aware of something they do not consciously know.

Some of the more significant studies regarding intuition have been conducted by Gary Klein, who developed the idea of recognition-primed decision-making (RPD). RPD describes how people with expertise intuitively identify a pattern in a situation and quickly determine a course of responses, without any analysis or comparing different courses of action. These intuitive decisions are very often right—but they are "good enough" solutions, not perfect solutions. Klein and his fellow researchers conducted studies with pilots, nurses, military leaders, chess masters, firefighters, and other experts in various fields and determined that, in most cases, these experts did not deliberate when reacting to a situation—they just acted. The type of intuitive decision-making that Klein describes is best done in the types of situations that are time constrained, high stakes, uncertain, and constantly changing. Sound familiar? These are the exact types of situations that Marines, police officers, and other security personnel experience daily. One of the key aspects of RPD is pattern recognition: "The basic aspect of recognitional decision-making is that people with experience can size up a situation and judge it as familiar or typical."[8] These individuals do it quickly: Fire-ground commanders make 80 percent of their decisions in less than one minute, medics make trauma treatment decisions in seconds, chess masters play moves in less than six seconds.[9] Consequently, those with experience growing up in tough, do-or-die neighborhoods often have great intuition about places like downtown Baghdad or Kabul.

Most Marines do not have sufficiently significant life experience to make decisions like experts. They don't have the knowledge and experience base for their intuition to be completely reliable. However, by constantly being aware, Marines can proactively take action before getting caught right of bang. This is why Cooper's Color Code is so important. Cooper's Color Code allows us to quantify a Marine's state of mind and gives us a target of awareness to aim for. Unfortunately, most situations don't lead Marines into

Condition Yellow, rather they push Marines directly into Condition Red, and sometimes even Condition Black.

We need to be in the Yellow state of mind, left of bang, to avoid the possibility of deterioration into the Black state if and when there is a right-of-bang event. The Marine Corps war lab endeavored to detail the qualities a Marine would need to reach and maintain a Yellow state of awareness. They wanted to determine how a Marine on patrol could take on the offensive mindset of a hunter instead of the defensive mindset of prey.

5. THE EXPERTS

Throughout 2007, the Marine Corps Warfighting Laboratory leveraged the experience of many civilian and military experts to design and structure the course that would become Combat Hunter. The program was designed to take the best and most basic skills of observation, hunting, and urban know-how and combine them to increase Marines' abilities to proactively identify threats on the battlefield. Three specific skills were identified and focused upon: enhanced observation, combat tracking, and combat profiling. Ultimately, the Marine Corps Warfighting Laboratory chose three experts to lead the development, expansion, and initial instruction of each of these specialties, the three pillars of Combat Hunter.

Ivan Carter, a big-game hunter from Africa, developed the observation portion of Combat Hunter. He recognized the foundation of every hunter is the ability to see his prey. He influenced the development of classes to teach effective observation techniques and how to better use both day and night optics.

David Scott Donelan, a former Rhodesian special forces operator, designed the combat tracking portion of Combat

Hunter. Combat tracking teaches Marines how to read and understand the physical terrain and identify the physical evidence individuals leave behind as they move through an environment. This skill allows Marines to pursue an armed enemy while gathering information to determine their future actions and intent.

Greg Williams, a former law enforcement officer, designed the combat profiling pillar of Combat Hunter. While combat tracking is focused on the physical terrain, profiling teaches Marines how to read the human terrain through an increased understanding of human behavior. This allows Marines to recognize the subtle aspects of human behavior to find the enemy hiding in plain clothes.

The integration of these three skills and concepts into military operations, whether in an insurgency or in a full-scale war, creates a more intelligent warrior capable of outthinking and outmaneuvering an enemy who seeks to blend in with his environment. The goal of Combat Hunter is to teach Marines how to separate the "sheep" (the unarmed civilians that populate the battlefield) from the "wolves in sheep's clothing" (the enemy). In a war in which our enemies do not wear uniforms and blend in with and exploit the local populace, the effort to locate and isolate the enemy can be challenging. Combat Hunter aims to train Marines to face this problem head on.*

6. IT WORKS

The Marine Corps' Combat Hunter course has trained thousands of Marines since its inception in 2007 and continues to provide Marines with the skills and the mindset to survive

*The ability to identify attackers hiding in the crowd is a skill that both our nation's security forces and civilians should possess. For further information about applying these observations to ensure safety in schools, the workplace, or in public places, visit: www. cp-journal.com/leftofbang.

in the complex, chaotic environments of Afghanistan. The course is taught in various places and schools throughout the Marine Corps, but mainly the program has been geared toward training Marines before deployment. Through the hard work and dedication of the program's enlisted and officer instructors, Combat Hunter has made an invaluable impact on the Marine Corps. What have the instructors and students all come to realize?

It Works.

Since the first Combat Hunter course was conducted in the fall of 2007, deploying forces have provided incredibly positive feedback. Four comments are typical:

1. "This is the best training I've received in my entire Marine Corps career."
2. "I wish this course was longer."
3. "Every Marine should receive this training," and
4. "I wish I had had this training before I last deployed."

Marines have eagerly reported that the increased awareness of both the physical and human terrain has alerted them to threats and has given them additional time to recognize the situation and take action against the enemy. As instructors, this is positive and encouraging; however, the second reality is humbling and fills us with remorse.

Marines often tell us that the material they learned during Combat Hunter could have helped them when they were in combat. Often, students remembering specific events reflect on a fallen brother- or sister-in-arms that might still be alive if they had received this training sooner. Unfortunately, not every Marine receives this training. This book on combat profiling and our training website are designed to supplement the Combat Hunter program and correct that problem. Every Marine and soldier should have this training before they deploy and must face an armed enemy.

The concept of Combat Hunter is a working hypothesis, not an established science. However, we have seen this concept work in practice and continually receive feedback from Marines deployed about the effectiveness of what we teach. The program works. It has made Marines more aware of their surroundings, more survivable, and more lethal on the battlefield.

Combat Hunter, and specifically combat profiling, is not solely for Marines. These concepts and lessons relate to every person who has dedicated his or her life to protecting others—soldiers, sailors, airmen, police officers, other security personnel, or even those who simply want to remain safe as they go about their daily lives. Whether you and your family are on vacation overseas or whether you are a woman who finds yourself alone in a dangerous environment, understanding when you or your loved ones are in potential danger can be the difference between life or death. Combat profiling is universal and applicable anywhere in the world.

7. WHAT COMBAT PROFILING IS

This book is focused on the Combat Hunter's third pillar, combat profiling, a method of proactively identifying threats based on human behavior and other cues from one's surroundings. Combat profiling is a practice based on a proactive mindset that incorporates many specific skills. Four of these are situational awareness, sensitivity of baselines and anomalies, critical thinking, and decision-making.

Combat profiling allows the Marine, soldier, or law enforcement officer to proactively identify threats based on human behavior. To do this, that operator must first be actively aware of his or her surroundings. The first skill this method provides is the ability to quickly develop situational awareness. To have situational awareness, you must be able to read both the environment and the people around you. However, you must also be able to separate important from unimportant information. Not everything you see is relevant for identifying threats.

The second skill in combat profiling is the ability to determine what indicators are important and directly related to your safety. This means being able to pick up on both overt and subtle cues of the physical environment and people's behavior. We will discuss human behavior further below and will provide detailed discussions of human behavior in the following chapters, but for now, it is sufficient to say that people's behavior betrays their intentions. By this, we mean that you can read subtle cues in a person's behavior to determine and predict what they will do. Combat profiling gives you both an in-depth understanding of human behavior and the skills to read human behavior and predict people's intentions. We will tell you what indicators to look for to identify threats, threatening behavior, and threatening environments.

The third skill that combat profiling teaches is critical thinking. We are surrounded by information, ambiguity, and various factors in different situations. No two situations are exactly alike. Therefore, we teach you how to critically assess the information you collect and how to weed out the unimportant information and focus on the important.

Finally, the fourth skill this method teaches is the ability to make sound snap decisions, or "heuristics." Heuristics are ways of making a decision with limited time and information. Whether you are in the military or law enforcement, you will never have all the time or information you need to make the perfect decision. So you must make the best decision with what you have. Unfortunately, few people are ever taught how to make a decision. Decision-making is either something you are assumed to have learned throughout life or are taught as a lengthy, deliberate process. Neither of these options helps the operator on patrol. So we teach you how to make an accurate decision quickly based on a few pieces of relevant information.

8. PROACTIVE, NOT REACTIVE

Combat profiling is, first and foremost, not racial profiling. When identifying threats, one does not focus on race, religion, or ethnicity, but on behavior within a given situation. In fact, someone who only focuses on surface, broad-based differences between humans is playing right into the hands of the enemy. The enemy has exploited those prejudices extremely effectively.

Unfortunately, since 2001, most Americans, including military and law enforcement personnel, have fallen victim to Islamophobia. We constantly look for people who look like "terrorists." By this, we implicitly mean young to middle-aged, Middle-Eastern, Muslim males. There are several problems with this. First, only a small percentage of Muslims are extremists, and only a small percentage of those individuals conduct violent acts. Second, criminals and terrorists come in all shapes, sizes, and ages and from all races, ethnicities, and religions. They can be either male or female. The United States has suffered enough from homegrown terrorists like Timothy McVeigh that we should know not to assume a person is a terrorist because of appearance. Third, as we will discuss later regarding decision-making, by focusing on indeterminate factors such as race or ethnicity, we miss out on important behavioral indicators that are necessary in identifying threats.

Additionally, when we allow our false, preconceived notions and biases to give us tunnel vision, we do not see the dangerous individuals who do not fit our "racial profile."

Combat profiling is also not criminal, psychological, or personality profiling. These types of profiling have specific purposes and are valid and useful within the appropriate contexts. A criminal profile is "a collection of inferences about the qualities of the person responsible for committing a crime or a series of crimes."[10] That is, criminal profiling is a way of "inferring the characteristics of an offender from the way that offender acted when committing the crime."[11] Criminal profiling analyzes the evidence and patterns of a particular perpetrator to infer certain personality characteristics to assist in solving crimes. This type of profiling is synonymous with what the FBI terms "criminal investigative analysis."[12] Although combat profiling shares several qualities with criminal profiling—like inference, critical thinking, analyzing patterns, and considering an individual's or group's *modus operandi* (MO)—the two methods differ significantly in their applications.

The first, and primary, difference between criminal profiling and combat profiling is that criminal profiling is reactive, while combat profiling is proactive. Since we are not yet at the point of precognitively seeing future crimes like in the movie *Minority Report*, criminal profiling requires that an individual commit a crime or a series of crimes to develop a profile of the perpetrator. Additionally, criminal profiling is a non-real-time, behind-the-scenes type of analysis. Unless specific evidence is available, criminal profiling cannot predict the time, location, and target of the next crime. Conversely, combat profiling is an on-the-spot method of proactively identifying and predicting a threat. It is used by individuals wherever they are, in real-time. While combat profiling does use information gained from previous attacks or crimes, similar to criminal profiling, the focus of combat profiling is to be proactive and prevent the event from ever occurring.

Now that we have a very broad understanding of what Combat Hunter is (proactive, behavior-based data collection and analysis) and isn't (prejudicial, socially imposed categorization with no analysis beyond black or white), what are the skills Marines learn in combat profiling training? What the experts have contributed has saved scores of Marines.

PART TWO

EVERYWHERE WE GO, THERE WILL BE PEOPLE

1. THE DILEMMA

On November 1, 2011, Marine 1st Lt. Jeff Waddell was on duty monitoring surveillance video when he spotted a known enemy operative. This insurgent was responsible for building the bomb that wounded a Marine sergeant two days before. 1st Lt. Waddell, a Bronze Star recipient from his previous deployment to Afghanistan, ordered a nearby sniper team to fire on the man after receiving permission from the battalion's combat operations center. After the snipers hit the insurgent, a group of Afghan males ran to the man and attempted to put him on a tractor. Seeing this, 1st Lt. Waddell ordered the sniper team to engage the tractor's engine block to disable it and prevent the man from escaping. The tractor was hit, and no civilians were injured. It wasn't until approximately three weeks later that it was discovered that the people who rushed out to help the wounded insurgent were teenagers. Upon this discovery, 1st Lt. Waddell's battalion commander promptly relieved him of duty for violating the rules of engagement because the snipers fired at individuals who were seemingly giving "medical assistance" to the wounded insurgent. Despite the positive review from a Marine brigadier general who stated that 1st Lt. Waddell was a "superb and heroic combat leader," his career was effectively stunted. Despite the fact that his quick, level-headed thinking dealt with the situation in a way that resulted in no civilian casualties, 1st Lt. Waddell was punished because of the complexity of the rules Marines must follow while overseas, the rapid pace of combat, and the difficulty of the decisions Marine leaders must make without access to complete or perfect information.[13]

There are several problems with the situations with which Marines are faced and the decisions they are forced to make. The first is that no one has ever taught Marines, or anyone really, how to make decisions—particularly quickly, with little time and information. Throughout life, people are expected to simply learn through trial and error how to make a decision. Generally, this tacit way of learning to make decisions is adequate to get most people through life, but in stressful situations such as combat, many people either freeze and make no decision or make terrible decisions.

Marines learn two lessons early on that give them a false sense of decision-making ability: BAMCIS and OODA. BAMCIS is a Marine Corps acronym for the six troop-leading steps:

- Begin the planning,
- Arrange the reconnaissance,
- Make the reconnaissance,
- Complete the plan,
- Issue the order, and
- Supervise.

Unfortunately, these "troop-leading steps" do not actually teach Marines how to make a decision. They outline a general process of developing and executing a plan. The second acronym, OODA, stands for

- Observe,
- Orient,
- Decide, and
- Act.

This is also called the Boyd Decision Cycle. This process, articulated by Colonel (Ret.) John Boyd, describes the four main steps that a person, group, or organization takes from observing a phenomenon to responding. This is a very helpful way to envision how people observe their surroundings (Observe), make sense of what they see (Orient), decide what to do (Decide), and then execute what they've decided (Act). However, just as BAMCIS simply tells a Marine to begin and complete a plan without teaching them *how* to plan, OODA states that a decision must be made without explaining how to make that decision or what Marines should be seeking to decide intelligently.

2. PARALYSIS BY ANALYSIS

The second problem is that the decision-making methods people are taught are almost exclusively analytical, very deliberate approaches of weighing the various issues to a problem (pros and cons, costs/risks and gains, etc.) and then, somehow, determining the best decision. Analytical decision-making works in situations in which:

- We need to make the best possible decision.
- We have sufficient time to problem solve, plan, and deliberate options.
- We have sufficient information to consider all the issues.
- We have clear criteria to decide between options.
- We need to justify our decision.
- We need to carefully plan contingencies or alternate plans.

Unfortunately, most situations Marines encounter do not allow for any analysis at all. While the analytical approach has its strengths, it also has its weaknesses. In fact, many of its strengths are often liabilities:

- Deliberate planning often takes too much time to conduct fully.
- There is often not enough information to analyze a situation or problem properly.
- Too much information exists without a way to determine what's most important.
- Clear criteria for choosing between options may not exist, or options may be similar enough that a deliberate decision is practically arbitrary.

The reality is that we don't use this approach for the majority of decisions we make on a daily basis. If we did, we would never get through the day. Imagine thinking through the issues, developing multiple options, weighing the pros and cons, and determining a course of action for everything we do. We have probably all seen someone fall victim to "paralysis by analysis" and become unable to make a decision because of his or her need to consider every piece of information.

Furthermore, even deliberate decision-making is not purely analytical in every way; it often uses intuition and heuristics. Last, just because a person uses analysis does not guarantee that the decision will work, be right, or even be good. Analysis is often wrong and in many cases ends up with less accurate decisions than either intuition or heuristics.

It isn't uncommon to think through something, only to have a gut feeling that the decision we made is not the right one. The problem for Marines is that analytical decision-making is neither practical nor useful in the high-stress situations encountered while on patrol: whether to shoot or not in a matter of milliseconds, whether to travel a particular stretch of road, whether to go on the alert when passing a group of villagers. A better, quicker method of making decisions is needed.

3. INFORMATION OVERLOAD

The next problem is a sort of a paradox. At one and the same time, Marines are bombarded with too much information and must make decisions based on too little information. Marines operate in 360-degree, three-dimensional environments, threatened by hazards from any direction. Anyone and anything could be a threat. Any trash pile could be hiding an IED. Furthermore, Marines are often doing multiple things at once: communicating with one another, maintaining their patrol formation, and providing security by watching their sector. Some are talking with locals, some are monitoring the radio and communicating with other units, some are specifically looking for certain types of threats (e.g., vehicle-borne improvised explosive devices [VBIEDs], snipers, IEDs). Meanwhile, each Marine is thinking through potential situations and attempting to determine how to react. The amount of information that Marines must try to process at any given time is overwhelming.

Marines never have enough information to make a perfect decision. Local drivers often speed toward a patrol oblivious to the patrol's presence. Unfortunately, to the Marines on patrol, this looks like the action of a suicide bomber. Locals often approach patrols with requests. Marines have no way of absolutely knowing any particular individual's intentions, whether hostile or friendly. The challenge of language and cultural barriers only compound the uncertainty and difficulty of determining a person's intentions. Despite this, Marines must make a decision; unfortunately, to wait until the speeding driver or the approaching local is definitively a threat will often be too late. Therefore, Marines must be taught a way to make decisions that ignores unimportant information while taking advantage of the little important information they do have.

4. PERFECT DECISIONS AREN'T POSSIBLE

Marines on the ground are often expected, though this is not explicitly stated, to make perfect decisions. A decision a Marine on the ground makes may carry significant, possibly even strategic level consequences, but it is simply impossible for Marines to make perfect or even the "best" decision in any given situation. The environment is too complex, time is too short, and not enough clear indicators are available. At the higher levels of command, it is widely recognized that leaders should not seek to make the perfect or best decision, but to make a good decision. In fact, General Patton is often quoted as saying, "A good solution applied with vigor now is better than a perfect solution ten minutes later."[14] One of the Marine Corps' own doctrinal publications states: "Many military problems simply cannot be solved optimally, no matter how long or hard we may think about the problem beforehand. In many cases, the best we can hope for is to devise partial, approximate solutions and refine those solutions over time, even after execution has begun."[15] Later, the same publication states, "What matters most is not generating the best possible plan but achieving the best possible result."[16] Leaders and planners are called to devise good enough solutions quickly, then aggressively carry out those solutions. The goal is to act violently and quickly to drive the tempo of battle and cause the enemy to react.

If leaders and planners are expected to make good enough, but not perfect, decisions, why are the Marines on the ground expected to make perfect decisions? Many Marines (as well as soldiers and police officers) have been second-guessed, investigated, and disciplined for making less than perfect decisions in the midst of a stressful, chaotic, uncertain, and time-constrained situation. The irony is that the leaders and planners who are expected only to make good-enough decisions have significantly more time and information to decide than the Marine on the ground. It is the Marine *on patrol*, surrounded by potential threats, who must be given the freedom and training to make good-enough decisions. This is not an argument for Marines to go out and make poor decisions. The purpose of this discussion is to point out that Marines are only able and should only be expected to make good-enough decisions. Therefore, Marines should be given the training to make quick, good-enough decisions, which will most often be the best decisions they can make.

A better way forward is needed. Marines must be given the tools to observe more acutely, judge more accurately, and decide more quickly in dynamic environments. This is where combat profiling fits in. The decision-making that Marines learn helps them to focus on the most important pieces of information and make accurate snap decisions based on that information. Marines learn to have a bias for action and be proactive in identifying and dealing with threats. Combat profiling teaches Marines a simple, yet effective strategy to use on the battlefield.

5. THE BETTER WAY

The combat profiling way of making decisions is the better way. Heuristics is nothing more than a way of making decisions with little time and information. Let me give a scientific definition and then provide a down-to-earth explanation. A heuristic is "a (conscious or subconscious) strategy that searches for minimal information and consists of building blocks that exploit evolved abilities and environmental structures."[17] In simple terms: Many problems and situations in life do not have perfect solutions, and the best solution is unknowable. Many situations are so complex, it is impossible to examine every piece of information—or so dangerous that looking for more than a few pieces of critical information risks lives.

In these situations, only the minimum amount of information is needed to make a decision. Often, just one piece of information, one cue, is important. A heuristic focuses on the important cue or cues and ignores the rest. A good heuristic decision is made by 1) knowing what to look for, 2) knowing when enough information is enough (the "threshold of decision"), and 3) knowing what decision to make.

A heuristic exploits our evolved capabilities—in the case of combat profiling, the ability to "thin-slice," quickly pick up on patterns, and determine a person's intentions based on human behavior. Thin slicing means making a determination about a situation or person with a thin slice of information, often with just seconds of observation.

But can quick observations be accurate?

More than 100 scientific studies have demonstrated that people can make incredibly accurate intuitive judgments with just a little amount of information.[18] These studies have researched a wide array of quick, accurate judgments made in a matter of seconds or minutes. For example, in just two seconds of observation, people can determine whether someone is a violent offender.[19] In determining whether someone is lying, fifteen seconds of observation are better than three minutes.[20] By looking at a group interacting for only thirty seconds, a person can accurately determine the role of each person in the group just based on body language and nonverbal signals. "From contexts as diverse as evaluating classroom teachers, selecting job applicants, or predicting the outcomes of court cases, human judgments made on the basis of just a thin slice of observational data can be highly predictive of later behavior."[21]

Army Sergeant First Class Tierney was on patrol in summer 2004 in Mosul, Iraq. He was leading his squad down a street when the patrol neared a car parked on the sidewalk. Inside the car were two young boys staring at the soldiers. The car was facing opposite the direction of traffic, and the windows were rolled up. It was 120 degrees that morning.

The soldier closest to the vehicle must have felt compassion for the two boys inside. If it was 120 outside, the inside of the car must have been a death trap. The soldier asked SFC Tierney if he could give the boys some water. Tierney said no and then told his men to fall back.

As soon as the soldier turned around, the IED exploded.

On this day, no soldiers were killed or severely wounded, because SFC Tierney listened to something inside him that said the situation wasn't right. Perhaps it was the fact that they were not greeted as usual by the locals when they left on patrol. Perhaps it was the fact that things seemed quieter than normal—no one had shot at them yet. Perhaps it was the fact that two children were inside a car—which must have been well over 120 degrees inside—with the windows rolled up. Whatever it was that tipped Tierney off, it wasn't rational analysis that made him suspicious. Call it a sixth sense, gut feeling or intuition; regardless, his brain was processing information and nudging him in a way that bypassed his conscious brain. Tierney says his body got colder. He called it the, "you know, danger feeling."[22]

One way the brain may drive these decisions is through the amygdala, a part of the limbic system that deals with emotion, memory, and decision-making. When a person encounters something that innately or through learning has emotional significance, they automatically experience an emotional response.[23] SFC Tierney had significant experience and training identifying IEDs and the warning signs of an attack. Although he did not explicitly or rationally think through all the factors that led to his decision, he nonetheless observed various indicators, which his brain was processing outside his conscious awareness, and then acted based on the emotional signals his brain was giving that things were not right.

Humans have evolved to make quick decisions, often based on patterns we have observed and learned: "If facing someone or something in the forest, our ancestors needed to respond instantly: friend or foe? Those who could read an expression in a flash more often lived to leave descendants, including us."[24] Intuition is best used when a person has significant experience and knowledge, which guides that person's subconscious thought processes. Where does this hinky mojo come from? The answer lies in millions of years of human evolution.

The Middle of Your Brain

Think back to the Stone Age. Our knuckle-dragging ancestors were both hunter and prey. They needed to forage for food, hunt, and bring home the bacon (so to speak) every single day. So, too, were they the main course for much larger and stronger mammals. It's safe to say that those human beings capable of avoiding being eaten were the ones able to procreate and pass their genes to the next generation of knuckle draggers.

Something inside those human brains gave them an advantage. What that something was and remains today lies inside the limbic system, the middle of our brains.

The front parts of our brains, above our eyeballs, defines the modern human. This frontal cortex is the place where thoughts, emotions, and senses are experienced and recorded. The middle part of the brain is the limbic system, the place where automatic behaviors live, including flinches, twitches, and for lack of a better description, our "extra senses," which tell us when something is not quite right. The last part of the brain is around the blood brain barrier, and this part is kind of the engine center. It keeps our heart going, keeps us breathing without thinking about it, etc. It's essentially our automatic systems coordinator.

The part of the brain that combat hunters need to trust in themselves and understand in others is the middle brain, known as the limbic system.

The Limbic System

To understand body language relating to behavioral analysis, it is critical to have a basic knowledge of the cognitive basis of nonverbal behavior. All our gestures, postures, and expressions result from the way our brain identifies and perceives threats, consciously or subconsciously. The most important part of the brain that directly affects nonverbal behavior is the limbic system. The limbic system is unique because, in addition to controlling emotions, it is completely focused on our survival.[25] Due to this important function, to ensure a person's protection from threats, it reacts to the surrounding environment automatically, immediately, and outside conscious awareness. Surviving in hostile, predator-filled environments requires immediate reaction, and the limbic system is designed to respond quickly and spontaneously. Therefore, the limbic system is also the honest part of the brain because it provides unmediated responses to external stimuli.

The limbic system is a team of structures in the brain (such as the amygdala, hippocampus, hypothalamus, and thalamus) that work together to ensure our survival. The limbic system processes information observed by the various senses (sight, sound, smell, taste, touch) and continuously and rapidly assesses that information in a very simplistic way, categorizing each stimulus as either a threat or a non-threat. To ensure an immediate reaction to a determination of "threat," the limbic system commands a response from the body that is instantly executed. The body will react to a threat by stopping in place and halting all movement, moving away from the threat, or preparing to physically engage the threat. These three responses are often referred to as the "freeze, flight, or fight" responses.

Freeze, Flight, and Fight

THE FREEZE RESPONSE

The freeze response is an early survival mechanism that is hard-wired into the brains of most creatures. Eyes are naturally attracted to movement, so the early ancestors of humans and other animals could escape detection from predators by simply freezing in place. In common terms, this equates to the "deer in the headlights" look.[26] Police officers have seen this response from foiled burglars who freeze in place before attempting to flee.[27] Freezing is a concept ingrained into Marines and soldiers who are taught to drop to the ground and freeze when flares or illumination go off in the middle of the night. By simply halting all movement, humans and animals increase the chances of not being seen and therefore increase the chances of survival.

This response also provides time to further assess the situation before executing the next decision, whether flight or fight. Physiologically, the brain also suppresses bodily functions such as heart rate, breathing, and blood pressure, and subdues those vital systems so the brain can take in as much information as possible before making a determination to stay and fight or flee.[28]

THE FLIGHT RESPONSE

The flight response is the second option the limbic system considers regarding survival. The purpose of fleeing is to create a physical separation from the predator or threat and thus avoid injury or death. The greater the distance from the attacker, the fewer options the attacker has to do harm and the more time the victim has to respond to further movements by the attacker. In most situations, however, humans cannot simply run from everything that is a potential physical or psychological threat, and so other distancing behaviors have developed to serve the same purpose, such as putting up a barrier, leaning away, covering the face, or turning one's back. Regardless of whether one runs from the threat or distances oneself nonverbally in some other way, the purpose of flight is to increase the distance from the attacker, and thus increase one's chance of survival. However, if fleeing isn't a viable option, almost all creatures will turn to the last response: fight.

THE FIGHT RESPONSE

The fight response is the last option considered by the limbic system because of the inherent potential for harm or death. The most ferocious fighters are vulnerable to injury from less dangerous creatures. This potential for harm makes fighting the least preferred response. However, before engaging in a fight, most creatures will attempt to persuade the other combatant to back down without physical confrontation. This is called posturing and is an attempt to win a fight without fighting. Posturing involves trying to appear larger and more dangerous and includes shouting, spreading the arms or other appendages wide, puffing up the chest to look larger, or moving around and taking up more space on the ground while appearing unpredictable. However, when a person's back is against the wall, either physically or psychologically, the brain willingly and quickly prepares the body to fight if that is the best chance for survival.

Why We Need This Information

Although there are few threats that we face in today's society that require us to respond with physically striking a person (fight) or physically fleeing from a person that intimidates us (flight), they still manifest themselves in various forms. Think of a situation that you have experienced recently where a person got too close to you and you felt that they had entered your "personal bubble." How did you respond to that invasion? If you took a couple steps away from them to re-establish that separation or even simply leaned back in your chair, you executed a form of the flight response. When we feel threatened, we will attempt to distance ourselves from that threat, even if it is only a few inches or feet. Think of another situation where someone challenged you about a topic about which you knew you were correct. How did you respond in this situation? Did you stand up, put your hands on your hips, gesture aggressively towards them, and raise your voice? Those dominant behaviors were driven by the same fight response used by people around the world in response to threats and stressful situations. The way that those responses manifest themselves in observable body language cues are how we can accurately apply these observations around the world.

Understanding the limbic system and its core freeze, flight, or fight responses is the first phase in detecting a threat. It's important to remember that the enemy stalking a Marine on patrol or a seemingly helpless woman on her way home is under duress. This stress manifests itself in physical actions. If we look for these particular physical actions when our limbic system gives us the "heads up, something's not right" signal, we'll be able to operate effectively "left of bang."

But once we start cataloging these behaviors to support our gut feelings, how do we decide when the evidence is overwhelming enough to act?

6. BIAS FOR ACTION

Combat profiling is a method of making decisions in complex, chaotic, hostile environments, where no perfect solutions exist, where decisions need to be made quickly and with little information, and where operators need to make the most of their intuition. Any method of making a decision in a combat environment should drive Marines to make a decision and quickly act on that decision—to maintain a bias for action. Combat environments, or any hostile environment for that matter, require people to be able to recognize threats and patterns quickly and then act immediately based on that information. "To hesitate is often to be lost, whether this means losing an opportunity for a meal or a mate to a competitor, or losing one's life or limb to a predator or otherwise hostile environment."[29] As we have already shown, researchers have demonstrated that "Good decisions can be made with little information."[30]

As we can see, it is incredibly helpful to have thick file folders locked inside the front part of our brains when making intuitive decisions influenced by our middle-brain limbic system.

But what about the vast majority of people who don't have the necessary life experience to take advantage of those decisions? When we do not have the experience necessary to quickly pick up on patterns and identify good-enough solutions immediately, we have to use another way to make quick decisions with little information. This is the benefit of the heuristic method used in combat profiling.

Combat profiling is heuristically and intuitively driven. It is built like a heuristic but applied with intuition. The basic foundation of combat profiling involves quickly establishing a baseline and determining anomalies, as well as quickly identifying threat indicators. Establishing a baseline involves observing only certain types of information, the information that comes from the six domains. Once an individual reaches the threshold of decision—identifying a certain number of anomalies or certain types of indicators—the individual must make a decision. Combat profiling drives individuals to have a bias for action.

Before the combat profiler can act and destroy the threat, he needs to detail and profile his target to support and determine his action. But for a combat profiler to identify the anomalies that influence his decisions, he needs to establish a baseline of behavior.

7. BASELINES AND ANOMALIES

"Well, the sheriff came around in the middle of the night / Heard mama cryin' / knew something wasn't right."

—Steve Earle, "Copperhead Road"

Humans effectively live because things generally remain the same. Traffic generally flows the same way, at the same time, on the same days. Our friends behave the same in similar situations. Life works because things have a "normal." But, when something is off, out of place, or unusual, we know that something isn't right. When "something isn't right"— whether the situation is a relationship, walking down the street, or on patrol in Afghanistan—then it's likely there is a problem. Unfortunately, most people don't do anything when "something isn't right." They don't allow their intuition to guide them. They don't proactively seek to determine what is out of place, they don't step back to observe the situation more closely, or they don't duck. It is only after the situation has occurred—in hindsight—when they realize something was out of place. This is living "right of bang."

In March 2011, the Second Reconnaissance Battalion sent out the daily patrol to provide route clearance and security for an engineering company that was doing road improvement in Helmand Province, Afghanistan. On this day, things weren't normal. For this province, normal meant people outside—people traveling, kids playing, people interacting. Normal included a man who would sit in front of his house drinking tea every day. This day, no one was outside, not even the daily tea drinker whose house was closed and locked. When something isn't normal, watch out. The abnormal atmosphere of the village—these anomalies— indicated what was to come. As the patrol moved forward, a

250-pound IED exploded beneath a 14-ton mine-resistant ambush protected (MRAP) vehicle, sending the vehicle flying into the air and injuring the Marines inside.[31]

Identifying threats means establishing a baseline and looking for anomalies. A baseline is what is normal for an environment, situation, or individual. Generally, every environment, type of situation, or individual exhibits normal patterns: patterns of movement, emotion, behavior, and interaction. We usually do not consciously consider what these patterns are because they are ingrained in us. While some of these patterns differ from culture to culture, place to place, or person to person, patterns are a part of life and human behavior around the world.

An anomaly is any variation from the baseline—and what we are primarily searching for is anomalies. Anomalies are things that either do not happen but should, or that do happen but shouldn't. During any situation, we expect certain things to happen and not to happen. For example, when a VIP (high-ranking military officer, village elder, etc.) walks into a room, we expect individuals to stand and greet the VIP; any variation from this (individuals not standing as the VIP enters or not greeting the VIP) is an anomaly. Anomalies indicate something has changed in the situation. Often they are indicators that something is awry. Another way to classify an anomaly is based on the presence or absence of something. When something (or someone) is not present when it should be, or is present when it shouldn't be, this is an anomaly. Now, it is normal for baselines to vary to some degree. Not every person wakes at the same time. Traffic patterns vary slightly from day to day and week to week. This is why we observe significant variation and look for multiple indicators that the baseline has changed. In a complex environment, one indicator is often not enough to act on.

Another way to describe the relationship between anomalies and the baseline is that anomalies are things that rise above or fall below the baseline. Anomalies that rise above the baseline are things that 1) are happening that shouldn't or don't normally happen or 2) are present that shouldn't be or aren't normally present. Anomalies that fall below the baseline are things that 1) are *not* happening that should happen or normally occur or 2) are *not* present that either should be or normally are present.

Anomalies that rise above the baseline

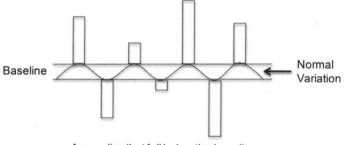

Anomalies that fall below the baseline

Why are anomalies indicators of potential threats? Anomalies are indicators of changes in situations. Granted, not every change in a situation is bad, but any change in a situation needs to be considered with suspicion. As we have already said, life works when things are normal. Humans, societies, nature, etc. fall into behavioral patterns. When something new is introduced into a situation, changes are evident. Whatever is new is an anomaly, and the resulting changes are anomalies because they differ from the baseline. For example, if a new person comes into an unfamiliar area, that person's actions will not be normal in relation to the locals because the person is unfamiliar with and/or uncomfortable in the area. Additionally, the locals will respond to the "intruder" in ways that are also abnormal—different than how they would interact with fellow locals.

The phrase "something wasn't right" is common lingo among people who have observed anomalies. People say it in hindsight about someone's behavior leading to suicide. Cops use it to describe suspicious behavior, which they might discover was indicative of a crime taking place or a perpetrator. In 2009, a University of California, Berkeley, police officer acted on a suspicion that "something wasn't right" and solved an 18-year-old kidnapping case.[32] What the officer observed was abnormal behavior from children a man claimed were his. Their behavior was emotionally unresponsive, eerie, and suspicious.

When trackers observe the ground for evidence of their quarry (the term for whatever they are following) they are looking for anomalies. The physical environment, like the social environment, has a baseline. Nothing in nature looks like a human footprint. Mud doesn't magically appear on rocks. Rocks don't move on their own. Trackers look for things like disturbances, displacement of natural items, and discoloration of vegetation and other natural items. Inherent in those words is the sense that something isn't right. Combat profilers also seek disturbances in the human environment. Like Newton's Third Law of Motion, human actions have reactions. Any abnormal behavior is an anomaly that will result in more anomalies. Combat profilers need to carefully observe for anomalies and act when they identify them. Thankfully, humans act in predictable and usual ways that can serve as a starting point for observing human behavior and establishing baselines.

8. HUMAN UNIVERSALS

Combat profiling works because human behavior is the product of and driven by human nature. The founding principle of combat profiling is that beneath the differences and idiosyncrasies of varying human cultures there remains a universal constant we call human nature. Irises widen due to certain stimuli, adrenaline flows, muscles tense or relax; we smile, we cringe, we bare our fangs. Every person in the world possesses universals that allow us to apply the principles of combat profiling consistently anywhere across the globe. The foundation of combat profiling is the universal similarities in humans, despite cultural differences.

Donald E. Brown, professor emeritus of anthropology at the University of California, Santa Barbara, has determined more than 400 universal individual and cultural behaviors and traits. He writes: "Human universals—of which hundreds have been identified—consist of those features of culture, society, language, behavior, and mind that, so far as the record has been examined, are found among all peoples known to ethnography and history."[33] According to Brown, human universals include such things as daily routines, aggression, gestures, and facial expressions.[34] Paul Ekman, a renowned psychologist and leading expert on micro-facial expressions and deception detection, has determined seven universal facial expressions of emotion.[35] Alex Pentland, director of Massachusetts Institute of Technology's (MIT) Human Dynamics Laboratory, has studied and written about what are called *honest signals*. Honest signals are biology-based cues that animals and humans demonstrate that can be used to reliably predict behavior.[36] Research is showing that humans across the globe are much more alike than we previously knew and wanted to believe. This is wonderful news for the combat profiler because he can apply these concepts and methods anywhere in the world and be alert to potential threats. Based on these assumptions, we have identified nine principles of human nature that directly apply to combat profiling.

1) Humans are creatures of habit.

In a study conducted by Northeastern University network scientists, it was determined that human behavior, regarding patterns of movement and mobility, is 93 percent predictable. By using information collected from cell phones, physics professor Albert-Laszlo Barabási determined that human movement patterns are predictable regardless of distance traveled or demographic categories (such as age, gender, urban versus rural, etc.).[37] In short, "humans follow simple reproducible patterns."[38] Not only do people follow patterns, but also humans are reluctant to change those patterns until the behavior becomes unproductive.[39] In fact, even if faced with clear failure, people often follow the same behavioral patterns in the hopes they will work again.

2) Humans are lazy.

Humans are generally lazy and will take the path of least resistance. Faced with two or more options, the human will generally take the easiest. Given the choice between walking one hundred meters through the grass from one point to another and walking five hundred meters around the grass along a sidewalk, humans will generally take the shortest path, even though it is not an official or authorized path.

3) Humans are lousy liars.

Humans have significant cognitive limitations. It has been shown that imposing cognitive load can help uncover liars. A liar must create a story and monitor the fabrication to ensure it *sounds* believable while attempting to maintain a believable *appearance*. While telling a lie, the liar must monitor the interviewer's reaction to assess how he or she is doing; the liar is also taxed mentally because a lie requires continuous effort whereas telling the truth is automatic. So as thoughtful questions are brought to the table, forcing the liar to spend more mental energy creating a lie and keeping the lies straight, the liar becomes vulnerable to leaking emotions and other indicators that can alert us to deception.[40] Additionally, humans cannot divide their attention well. The more tasks a person divides his attention between, the poorer he will perform any of those tasks. Another example is short-term memory. Humans can only remember, on average, between five to nine items using their short-term memory. All of this is important because, as we observe individuals, reliable nonverbal indicators will leak out and indicate their emotions, attitudes, and intentions, particularly when their attention is focused on something such as completing their mission, getting close to their target, thinking about their next lie, etc.

4) Humans will run, fight, or freeze.

Humans are driven by fight-or-flight responses, which translate into certain autonomic responses and behaviors. We will discuss these responses later as well as the autonomic responses to stress. For now, it is sufficient to say that our bodies often exhibit uncontrollable, automatic reactions to our emotions in response to the situations we are in. Because these reactions are automatic and uncontrollable, they are reliable indicators of the emotions and attitudes of a person and can clue us in to how that person is feeling in any given situation. Furthermore, when we understand the fight-or-flight response, we can predict a person's behavior in any stressful or threatening situation.

5) Humans telegraph their intentions.

Emotions are difficult to control and are often spontaneous responses to a situation. As Paul Ekman points out, we don't often have control over our emotions, and our cognitive brain is not always in control of our emotions—at least at first.[41] By understanding the behaviors associated with specific emotions, we can identify people's emotional states and changes in relation to their emotions. As Alex Pentland discusses, "honest signals" are behaviors mainly driven by the subconscious. By reading people's honest signals, we can predict what people will do.[42] On a small scale, we see this principle play out in boxing and basketball. Good boxers can pick up on the ways their opponent telegraphs his next move. In basketball, good defenders look for ways in which their opponent telegraphs their next move, whether the player intends to go to the right, pass the ball, or take the shot. Poker players look for "tells" in their opponents' behavior. Combat profilers look for people telegraphing intentions to do harm.

6) Humans are predictable.

Humans are not generally spontaneous or random. This principle is related to the second principle above. As much as we think we are unpredictable and random, we really are very predictable and follow regular patterns. A study that tracked 10,000 people via cell phone concluded that people display a very high degree of regularity when they travel, because they return to only a few, very frequented locations.[43] A more mundane example is the game Rock, Paper, Scissors. Research shows that, even in games that rely on being unpredictable, humans are, in fact, very predictable and not at all random. We involuntarily mimic others, and we predictably attempt to come back from losses—at least in

Rock, Paper, Scissors—by doing whatever beat us in the last round.[44] This means that our enemy will set patterns that, if we take the time to analyze, we can identify and use to our advantage. Once we know the enemy's pattern, we can practically predict his next move. Unfortunately, this also means that we are not as random as we think and that the enemy can identify our patterns to predict our next movements and actions. Anyone who has operated in Afghanistan or Iraq can verify this reality: the enemy places the same type of IED in the same locations because we use the same routes at the same times. What we need to realize is that the enemy is also using the same routes, the same hiding places, and is conducting the same activities at the same times.

7) Humans are not good at multitasking.

In general, humans only look natural when naturally focused on doing one thing. Furthermore, multitasking is a myth. This relates to the principle above that humans have significant cognitive limitations. People can only do one thing at a time well; when they attempt to do more than one thing at a time, focus, ability, and productivity suffer. When your attention is divided, and you're concentrating on doing more than one thing, your behavior and speech will appear unnatural. For instance, if someone is actually reading a paper, then their attention and mental energy will be focused on reading the paper. If, however, that person is only acting as if they are reading the paper and instead is attempting to conduct surveillance, then that person's behavior will not look natural. Or imagine, for instance, conversing with someone attempting to discreetly watch someone in the crowd of people around you to get some type of subtle direction from that person. The person to whom you are talking will not be focused on the conversation. Instead, his mental energy will be divided. His action will be jerky, and his speech will seem choppy, broken, or slower than normal. His brain will have to switch back and forth between activities.[45]

As Alex Pentland explains, "When there are several conflicting 'commands' coming down from our higher brain centers, each requiring our body to take different sorts of actions, this interferes with our ability to act in a smooth, consistent manner."[46] He calls this aspect of behavior *consistency*.

8) Humans are generally clueless.

Humans in general lack situational awareness. As you go about your day, take a minute and simply watch the people around you. Generally, people walk with their heads down, or they are focused on one particular thing. People rarely look around at their surroundings (with two exceptions: good guys and bad guys. And even then these two types of people become focused and lose their general awareness at times). If they are looking around, they usually don't pick up on what is happening around them. Often, when conducting our own observation training off base, we establish overt observation posts on the top-floor balconies of buildings, or we sit in the open to observe a particularly busy location, often for long durations (several hours). We often begin by discreetly watching the behavior of people around us, in an attempt to pick up on behavioral patterns while not drawing attention to ourselves. However, after some time, we are usually blatant in pointing out observations—we often end up literally pointing. Particularly in today's security-concerned environment, you would assume that someone would confront us for "conducting surveillance." However, rarely does anyone even look at us, let alone think we are doing anything unusual. Yet, we are doing the exact same thing that a criminal or terrorist would do in preparation for a crime or an attack—and we aren't even attempting to disguise our behavior. Furthermore, because of our cognitive limitations, when a person is mentally focusing on something—whether an activity, conversation, or thought—they lose sense of their surroundings.

9) *Humans can't do very many different things.*

There are a limited number of dimensions in human behavior. Human beings are finite creatures. Our bodies react in certain ways to stress and other stimuli. Our communication is limited, basically, to verbal and nonverbal. We rarely act in isolation; rather, we interact with the environment around us.

Although there are a number of ways to view human behavior, we break human behavior into six different, but interrelated, dimensions (we call these the Six Domains.) These domains range from autonomic to deliberate, and personal to social. They are:

a. Kinesics: Conscious and subconscious body language.
b. Biometric Cues: Biological autonomic responses.
c. Proxemics: Interpersonal spatial interaction.
d. Geographics: Patterns of behavior within an environment.
e. Iconography: Expression through symbols.
f. Atmospherics: Collective attitudes that create distinct moods within an environment.

Combat profiling is based on these domains.

PART THREE

DETAIL

HEADLINE
TAKEN FROM NEWSPAPERS
ON JANUARY 1, 2000:

"Explosion at LAX, Millennium Bomber kills
over 100; over 300 injured"

But a bomb didn't explode on January 1, 2000, at LAX. No one's New Year's Day was interrupted by breaking news of hundreds dead. No one read this horrible headline. New Year's Day in 2000 did not become an American tragedy because of one person's suspicious behavior and one customs agent's quick thinking. In fact, September 11, wasn't supposed to be the opening salvo of Al-Qaeda's attack on the West. A year and a half before September 11, before the War On Terror became a frequent conversation at America's dinner tables, a 130-pound bomb was set to detonate on a luggage carousel at Los Angeles International Airport (LAX). The only reason that headline was never written was because of a woman named Diana Dean.

Dean was a customs agent at Port Angeles, WA, and was an inspector for people crossing into America on a ferry from Victoria, British Columbia. On December 14, 1999, just before 6 p.m., she approached the last car she was to inspect that day. As she took the driver's license and passport from a man she believed to be Benni Noris, she immediately realized something was wrong. There was something about Noris that Dean later described as "hinky." She couldn't figure out exactly what was wrong, but he wasn't acting like the other people she had inspected throughout her career. As she asked fairly simple and straightforward questions about where he was going and how long he planned on staying in the country, he became extremely fidgety and jittery, began to sweat, and seemed unnecessarily anxious—there was something not quite right about Noris or the way he was moving around inside his car.

Because of the man's suspicious behavior, Dean conducted a search on his rented 1999 Chrysler 300M, which should have been fairly simple because it was already searched as it was loaded on the ferry in British Columbia. As she went through the trunk of the car with the help from some other inspectors, she found many green plastic bags filled with a powdery substance underneath the cover to the spare tire compartment. There were also some black boxes, two pill bottles, and two jars with brown liquid in them. Their first assumption was that Noris was trying to smuggle drugs into the country.

The plan was to confront Noris with what they found, and as one inspector began to guide him to his car, Noris shuddered. Before they got to Noris' car, he took off running into the Port Angeles parking lot. When they finally detained him, it didn't take long for the customs agents to learn his real name was not Benni Noris and those weren't narcotics in his car trunk. The person they caught on December 14, 1999, was Algerian-born Ahmed Ressam, and the green bags were more than 130 pounds of explosive material. The Al-Qaeda-trained operative was on his way to Los Angeles to conduct surveillance on LAX for two weeks and to execute his strike on New Year's Eve.

What would have happened if Dean hadn't noticed the cues that something was wrong with Ahmed Ressam and that his behavior was outside the baseline she had established? She didn't use the terminology we discuss in this book, but she observed his kinesic cues, realized they were off, and took action. This happened 21 months before September 11, before there were legitimate concerns that Americans could be attacked at home. Her observations helped stop the "Millennium Bomber" from reaching his target and conducting a terrorist attack on American soil two weeks "left of bang."[47]

1. THE SIX DOMAINS

To make quick decisions, combat profilers need to know what to look for. Current battlefields bombard operators with massive amounts of information. Without the ability to filter out the nonsense and noncritical information, Marines and soldiers cannot effectively identify threats. Combat profiling focuses on the important details of human behavior, which can be viewed from six basic viewpoints. We label these dimensions the six domains.

First Domain: Kinesics...
is the domain that involves people's conscious and subconscious body language. This is important because humans give off signals through their postures, gestures, and expressions that communicate their current emotions and possibly their future intentions. Being able to pick up on these signals is critical to proactively identifying threats. See the section titled "kinesics" for an explanation of our use of the term.

Second Domain: Biometric cues...
is the term we use to describe the uncontrollable and automatic biological responses of the human body to stress. These physiological responses are key to understanding a person's emotional states and changes.

Third Domain: Proxemics...

is the domain that allows us to understand groups of people by observing interpersonal distance and identify an individual's relationships and intentions based on how they use the space around them. While proxemics is often discussed within the larger category of nonverbal communication, we separate it from biometrics and kinesics because proxemics allows us to understand an individual's behavior as it relates to the surrounding people. Proxemics also permits us to understand group dynamics.

Fourth Domain: Geographics...

is the domain that involves reading the relationship between people and their environment. This helps us to understand and identify who is familiar or unfamiliar with the area they are in and how people move around their surroundings. Because human behavior is predictable, combat profilers can anticipate where people will go and what they will do in certain areas.

Fifth Domain: Iconography...

is the domain that allows us to understand the symbols people use to communicate their beliefs and affiliations. Gangs, insurgents, terrorist groups, and individuals use iconography as a symbol of group unity, for rapid recognition of other members, and to communicate their beliefs to the larger populace. Observing these symbols, particularly the increased presence or even sudden absence of them, can be key to a combat profiler's situational awareness.

Sixth Domain: Atmospherics...

is the domain focused on the collective attitudes, moods, and behaviors in a given situation or a place. Combat profilers can read the social or emotional atmosphere of an environment and pick up on the changes or shifts in that atmosphere that often signal that something significant has changed or that something is about to occur. Understanding the collective atmosphere can key combat profilers into those individuals whose attitude, emotions, and behavior do not fit the given situation—these individuals are anomalies.

These six domains capture the most significant aspects of human behavior in simple terms that aid combat profilers in establishing baselines and identifying anomalies.

2. THE LANGUAGE OF PROFILING

We'll be the first to admit that this terminology is a mouthful. And the terms are not easily discernible to the average person either. However, by using the terminology of the domains and breaking nonverbal communication into its subcomponents, a police officer can effectively explain a decision to stop and search a person to his boss without being too specific. He witnessed a proxemic push (as the person tried to avoid his patrol), a biometric cue (the individual's hands began to shake when questioned), and kinesic indicators (the person began patting and touching his waistband). These observations would lead an officer to believe the person had a concealed weapon and would be able to confirm his assessment by searching the individual.

By adding a degree of descriptiveness and quantifying specifically what was observed, the police officer can be confident in his decision because it was based on grounded observations regarding the suspect's behavior, not inaccurate racial, gender, age, or religious biases.

When it comes to a person's ability to read body language, there are two types of people. The first is the person who was forced to learn the skill early in life because recognizing threats through behavior became the best chance for survival. People who grew up in dangerous neighborhoods or in abusive households had to learn to identify threats, or they paid the price for missing these signals. The second group of people learned somewhere later in life and probably learned through dedicated self-study. In American schools, we are taught to read, write, and speak English, but are never taught how to read body language. Because the people in this group are likely not the "naturals," they need a structure for consolidating the material and experiences they are using to develop themselves. The domains provide this framework.

We live in an age of information overload, and observing human behavior is no different. Although the terminology we use may seem foreign, it gives combat profilers an accurate and sufficiently specific set of terms to focus their observations, rapidly categorize what they observe, make good decisions quickly, and effectively communicate those observations to others. Combat profilers use the six domains to focus their observations on what is most important: human behavior.

3. KINESICS

"Everything a person does is created twice—once in the mind and once in its execution—ideas and impulses are pre-incident indicators for action."
—*Gavin de Becker*

Kinesics is the study of body language and accounts for a significant part of all interpersonal communication. Our use of the term kinesics may seem too general. For example, we could refine our discussion even further by differentiating between body movements (kinesics proper) and nonverbal communication that involves touching ("haptics"). However, incorporating additional teriminology would create unnecessary distinctions and would hamper rapid observation and effective communication. The purpose of our categories—the six domains—is to provide accurate and funtional language for individuals to make accurate observations and communicate those observations effectively. Although the term kinesics was originally coined by the anthropologist Ray Birdwhistell in the 1950s, it is still used by contemporary researchers and provides an accurate way to describe the movements of the limbs, head, and torso. Studying body language accomplishes two objectives. The first is to identify those people who don't fit in and thus warrant further attention. The second is to predict people's behavior based on the subtle behavioral cues that give away their intentions. These subtle and subconscious acts, rather than obvious movements, matter the most. When compared to the behavioral baseline, smaller signals often provide the information needed to make smarter, faster decisions in combat.

While researchers disagree as to what percentage of total communication is accounted for by body language and other nonverbal means, there is no doubt that a significant portion of all communication is transmitted nonverbally. To ignore such a significant aspect of communication would be foolish. Marines and other security personnel consistently interact with people from other cultures, many of whom do not share the same language. It is more important than ever to effectively read a person's intentions through body language and other nonverbal signals.

The science of body language can be used to separate the sheep from the wolves in sheep's clothing. Several critical issues guide the framework of this part of the book:

1. This is a chapter on body language. Numerous scholarly and popular resources exist on the topic of body language and nonverbal communication, including book-length treatments and extensive articles. The purpose of this discussion of kinesics is to emphasize the use of behavioral clusters and to describe how using clusters enables combat profilers to quickly and confidently interpret body language.

2. Most gestures, in and of themselves, are not important. What's important to the combat profiler is a gesture in the context of the baseline.

3. Combat profiling focuses on clusters of behavior, or multiple cues, rather than single gestures.[48]

4. All the information provided in this chapter will be about observable indicators below the shoulders. Understanding individual behavior is the foundation for combat profiling, and to do this accurately we will ignore facial communication.

Because of these reasons, this chapter does not discuss individual gestures. Instead, combat profiling relies on observing "clusters," which are groups of reinforcing gestures and other nonverbal indicators that communicate the same message. These clusters are then compared to the baseline to identify anomalies.

Why Not the Face?

The human face is incredibly expressive and is used both consciously and subconsciously in communicating emotion. In all six of the possible clusters that will be discussed below, facial expressions and emotions could be used to confirm and supplement the behaviors listed; however, facial expressions have been left out due to some inherent limitations.

The first limitation is that, to identify facial expressions accurately, you must be relatively close to the person you are observing. This can be useful in a setting such as an interview or conversation, but not necessarily in situations in which some type of safety standoff is required. Marines should be capable of recognizing and identifying kinesic clusters up close, but more importantly from longer distances for security and safety reasons. Since we discuss clusters without referring to facial expressions, we have given combat profilers the ability to determine people's emotions based on behavior indicators, which can be observed from a distance. However, facial expressions can still provide a significant amount of information to a combat profiler and should be observed to supplement the information garnered by observing the body language related to the clusters.

The second limitation to facial expressions is that a true emotion, which could be displayed as a micro-expression, may only be present on the face for 1/25th of a second. With an emotion displayed for such a short amount of time, there is a high chance that a Marine on patrol in a combat zone will miss it with so many other actions taking place around him. Just as with the first limitation, this does not mean Marines and other security personnel shouldn't be trained to identify these expressions since they can be some of the most honest indicators available, but operators need other indicators that may be present for a greater length of time.[*]

Universal Behaviors and Clusters

Because Marines operate throughout the world, combat profiling focuses on body language and analysis that is universally applicable, as opposed to country- or culture-specific gestures. Freeze, flight, and fight responses drive these types of universal behaviors.

---

*To learn about how to read facial expressions, visit: www.cp-journal.com/leftofbang

Since the field of kinesics was first studied, researchers have disputed the science behind body language because they cannot assign *one and only one* universal meaning to a specific gesture. For example, the simple behavior of crossing one's arms across the chest could mean several different things depending upon the context:

a. The person is cold and seeks to warm himself by crossing his arms.

b. The person is creating a barrier between him and someone else in an attempt to close himself off.

c. The person is comfortable and has crossed his arms because there is nothing else available to support or do with his arms.

d. The person is uncomfortable and is subconsciously attempting to protect himself.

To overcome this inherent ambiguity, combat profiling relies on brain science to determine the cause of these gestures. The body's reactions to our freeze, flight, and fight response provide us with a scientific cause for the gestures we are observing.[49] Furthermore, combat profiling relies on identifying clusters of mutually reinforcing cues to determine a person's intentions—these are groups of behaviors and gestures that point to the same meaning.

Combat profiling strives to observe clusters of multiple cues that lead to the same conclusion about what a person may be feeling or what his or her intentions are.[50] The more indicators leading to the same conclusion, the more accurate combat profilers will be in predicting a person's emotions and actions. To confirm a cluster, one needs to observe at least three indicators. Clusters are based on a person's perception of threats and how they are preparing to deal with them.

They are:
1. Dominant vs. submissive
2. Uncomfortable vs. comfortable
3. Interested vs. uninterested (in the person or object they are interacting with)

Looking back at how Dean initially described the Millennium Bomber's behavior provides one example for why we rely on these six classifications to describe the people around us. What she accurately described as "hinky" could have also been classified as anxious, nervous, suspicious, furtive, or any other synonym that a person could use to explain that type of behavior. We call that type of behavior "uncomfortable" to simplify how combat profilers communicate what they are observing. By ensuring that everyone is using the same terminology and language to describe and communicate their observations, we can also ensure quick, concise, and accurate discussions and decisions between everyone involved.

Once three indicators are observed, combat profilers then judge the cluster against the baseline: Should the person be feeling dominant/submissive, uncomfortable/comfortable, and interested/uninterested right now? If the person's behavior fits the baseline, then they do not require further investigation. However, if the person's emotions and behavior do not fit the situation, that person has now become an anomaly, and a decision must be made for dealing with that person. In the case of the Millennium Bomber, a certain degree of discomfort could be expected. Similar to passing through a TSA checkpoint at the airport, people may naturally exhibit a moderate amount of uncomfortable behavior solely because of the nature of the search. Ressam's intense, uncomfortable cues compared to other people Dean had searched (the baseline) alerted her to the anomaly.

There are, of course, an infinite number of ways to classify behavior; the clusters and categories used in combat profiling are quick, effective ways to assess people's behavior and identify potential threats.

The Dominant Cluster

The first cluster that should raise a combat profiler's awareness is the dominant cluster. Dominant behavior is an expression of the limbic system's fight response. Even in situations in which physical aggression is inappropriate, people often use dominant behaviors to intimidate, bully, and assert control over others. The rule used to classify a person as exhibiting dominance is that they are using their body to take up a greater amount of space or in a territorial display. Generally speaking, authoritative people seek to establish ownership over people and objects in their immediate vicinity,[51] and this begins with taking ownership of the space around them. Dominant behavior includes gestures and postures that make a person look larger to intimidate "smaller" people into submission. Examples of these gestures and postures include:

Lower Body:
1. Seated—Feet planted on floor, and legs splayed out, taking up space.[52]
2. Seated—Legs crossed and with their hands holding their ankle or lower calf, demonstrating confidence in one's view.
3. Standing—legs shoulder-width apart, taking up more space.

Torso:
1. Seated—Leaning back with hands clasped behind head, taking up more space.[53]

2. Standing—with hands on their hips in an authoritative way, with their arms akimbo they are taking up more space.[54]

3. Standing and leaning forward in an aggressive manner, attempting to look bigger or intimidate others.

4. Standing—Stretching torso and making oneself look taller by standing upright and erect.

5. This can be complemented by observing the chin up and thrusting the chest out.

Hands and Arms:

1. Arms spread out on an object (table, counter, etc.)—taking up more space, which is often considered a territorial display.[55]

2. Hands clasped behind back as if judging or evaluating.[56]

3. Wrist and palm facing down when shaking hands or greeting.[57]

4. Pointing with hands while talking or lecturing.[58]

5. Steeple gesture with hands (perceived as intellectual and confident).[59]

Other Indicators:

1. Maintaining one's gaze for a longer period of time, or not averting one's own gaze.[60]

2. Dominant people can breach others' intimate proxemic zone (discussed in a later chapter), showing they feel they can go wherever they want.

3. Touching other people which demonstrates control over another person.[61]

The Submissive Cluster

The submissive cluster is the opposite of the dominant cluster and is characterized by the absence of the fight response. This isn't to say that the person doesn't perceive a threat, only that the person has determined the best chance of survival against an aggressor is submission—literally, not putting up a fight or defending themselves. Submissive behavior is identified by the types of behavior that cause a person to take up less space. This is also a posture that can be used to show receptiveness, warmth, and respect. Indicators for submissive body language could include body language from the following list:

Lower Body:
1. Seated—feet and legs crossed at the ankle and tucked underneath the chair, making a person look smaller.
2. Seated—feet wrapped around legs of chair, seeking stability and security.[62]
3. Legs will often not be used as barrier as it could offend the dominant person or be seen as an aggressive response.

Upper Body:
1. Leaning forward apologetically and making the body smaller and less threatening, instead of the aggressive posturing forward lean of the dominant cluster.[63]
2. Arms pulled into the body (nonthreatening, no ability to strike back).[64]
3. Wrists and palms exposed in greeting (vulnerable).[65]
4. Shoulders lowered and not protecting the neck.[66]

Other Indicators:

1. Averting eyes or failing to make eye contact with another person.

Oftentimes people display submissive behavior when they are feeling nonconfrontational. Think about times in your life when you saw a person walking aggressively down the street and you stepped aside to let them by. As you are beginning to see, the behaviors that make up the clusters are ones that you have observed in other people or experienced yourself. Assigning names to the primary ways a person responds to stress is the first step in recognizing another person's emotional state.

It Isn't Always A Bad Thing—Keeping It In Context

The importance of putting observations into the context of their surroundings can't be overstated. Because Marines must quickly and accurately read those around them and determine if they are a threat or not, the clusters of dominance and submission are best described from the perspective of whether a person will put up a fight if confronted. The same dominance and submission cues can be also observed in other, nonhostile settings in which a subordinate person is showing a true level of respect and deference to a person of a higher status. In a case like this, the behavior for respect may be characterized as submissive, but the relationship isn't adversarial. Similarly, leaders accustomed to being in charge and having influence may naturally assume dominant postures when around others. Because dominance and submissiveness may have differing meanings in different situations, it is critical that combat profilers consider the context of the behavior.

The Uncomfortable Cluster

When a person feels threatened, scared, nervous, or begins to experience some other negative emotion, that person will display discomfort. This is part of the second category of clusters that combat profilers attempt to identify. Just as dominant behavior resulted from the limbic system's fight response, uncomfortable behavior comes from a person's flight response. People who perceive a threat will either want to remove themselves from the situation or do something to protect themselves. Distancing behaviors, using barriers, and pacifying behaviors are clear indicators that someone is uncomfortable. However, any combination of three indicators from the following list should immediately identify someone as uncomfortable.

Lower Body:

1. Feet bouncing (limbic system preparing the body for flight).[67]
2. Feet oriented toward a door or exit (showing what one's intentions are, preparing for flight).
3. Legs crossed while seated, forming a barrier (protecting vital areas).[68]
4. Legs shoulder width apart while standing (body capable of defending itself).[69]

Upper Body:

1. Torso leaning away (distancing from a threat).[70]
2. Torso rotated away from person or object (either facing exit to prepare for flight, or turning to protect vitals).[71]
3. Arms crossed across chest (establishing barriers to protect vital areas).[72]
4. Arms/hands covering crotch/groin (establishing barriers to protect vital areas).[73]

5. Shoulders raised (response to a threat to protect neck/carotid artery and head).[74]

6. Increase use of pacifying behavior (resulting from the energy manifested by the autonomic nervous system).[75]

Other Indicators:

1. Eyes glancing around the room, looking for an escape.

Pacifying Behaviors

The use of pacifying behaviors is an immediate sign someone is uncomfortable.[76] A pacifying behavior is any act or gesture used to calm or comfort oneself when experiencing the body's autonomic responses to stress. Different books and researchers may classify them using different terms, such as adaptors or self-manipulators,[77] but they all refer to the same category of gestures.* People display pacifying behaviors in different ways. Some people will clench their fists, some will rub their hands on their thighs, others will rub the bridge of their nose, and others will use a long, drawn-out exhalation to calm and compose themselves.

The cause of this type of behavior is initially triggered by the limbic system because the energy the autonomic nervous system is generating cannot always be used in overtly aggressive or protective ways, such as punching or fleeing. When someone experiences an increased heart rate or respiration rate (or any other limbic system response to a threat or stress), that person's body will respond to decrease heart rate and respiration. Pacifying behaviors allow the

---

*We have chosen the classification and terminology Joe Navarro uses in his book because, to us, it makes the section title "Pacifying Behavior" the most self-descriptive.

body to return to balance and release this built-up energy in discreet, comforting ways. This buildup of nervous energy is what drives pacifying behaviors.

The Comfortable Cluster

The comfortable cluster is the opposite of the uncomfortable cluster and is classified as the absence of the fight-or-flight response. No stimulus, whether a person or object, has caused the person to feel threatened. When a person feels safe, that person will display behaviors that indicate varying levels of comfort, vulnerability, and ease. A person who does not perceive any threat to his survival will display some of the behaviors listed below. Again, always look for clusters of three:

Lower Body:
1. Feet motionless and relaxed (no limbic system response causing them to distance themselves from the threat).
2. Legs uncrossed or legs crossed with the inside of the thigh exposed to another person (no limbic system response to protect vital areas and the femoral artery on the inside of the thigh).[78]
3. Standing with legs crossed (no threat perceived, body vulnerable while standing with all the weight on one foot, body not prepared to fight/flight).[79]

Upper Body:
1. Torso upright or leaning in (no threat perceived, not concerned about distancing).[80]
2. Torso leaning away or splayed out (in a reclined or lounging type manner, body unprepared to defend itself).[81]

3. Arms open—at the sides of the body, gesturing openly, or behind back (no immediate threat recognized and no need to use hands/arms to protect the body).[82]
4. Shoulders lowered—no turtle effect (no threat recognized, no need to protect vital areas of neck).[83]
5. No pacifying behaviors.

Other Indicators:
1. General relaxed postures.

Mutually Exclusive

The first four clusters that we discussed relate solely to a person's limbic system response to the world. Because a person cannot experience both a fight and flight response simultaneously, a person can only display one cluster at a time. This isn't to say that a person cannot escalate from uncomfortable behavior to dominant behavior very quickly, but the initial classification will be one or the other. The next category of clusters, interested vs. uninterested, complements the previous sets of clusters. An individual may be "dominant and interested" or "dominant and uninterested." Determining a person's interest will provide a great deal more information about the person's emotional state and future intentions.

The Interested Cluster

The third category of behavior clusters relates to a person's interest. The guiding principle for identifying a person's interest is assessing where the person's attention is focused, whether on the subject with whom they are interacting or elsewhere. Being able to determine who is interested or uninterested can provide a significant advantage when determining whom to contact and engage in conversation. Indicators that show if a person is interested can include:

Lower Body:
1. Feet pointing at people in conversation (both feet).[84]
2. Feet remaining still, not bouncing (no limbic system preparation to leave).
3. No leg barriers (openness).

Upper Body:
1. Torso leaning forward (seated or standing).[85]
2. Open body language (no arm barriers).[86]

Other Indicators:
1. Head nods.[87]
2. Gaze will be oriented in the direction of the person speaking.[88]
3. Mirroring or mimicking of any emotion communicated through the conversation by the other people in the group.

The Uninterested Cluster

The uninterested cluster will mainly be displayed through behaviors that demonstrate the person wants to leave the situation. These will include the following:

Lower Body:
1. Feet bouncing (body preparing to distance itself from the person or object).[89]
2. Feet oriented away from the person or object in the direction they would like to move.[90]
3. Legs crossed—use of leg barriers.
4. "Shifty" behavior, person moving or rocking back and forth.

Upper Body:
1. Arm barriers up (closing off front of torso).
2. Torso leaning away from person or object.[91]
3. May see "stopping" gestures with hands.
4. Increase use of pacifying behavior.

If a person displays any behavioral indicators of disinterest, that person's interest in a situation, conversation, or event is either waning or lost.

Emblems

Everything discussed to this point has been universal behavior, as it is driven subconsciously by the limbic system. There are also culturally specific kinesic cues that should be considered while preparing to deploy to a foreign country. One specific set of important and culturally specific behaviors is called "emblems." Emblems are hand gestures that can *replace* words.[92] Gestures used to communicate messages such as "stop" or "come here" are emblems. Other emblems include the "thumbs up," the "A-OK" sign, or the middle finger. Emblems can include facial actions and expressions such as nodding to show agreement and approval, or shaking the head to display disagreement and disapproval. Many emblems are displayed subconsciously and are very reliable indicators of the person's emotional state, particularly in settings in which a person must conceal his or her emotions. The topic of emblems is worth mentioning since they are significant and specific to each culture. However, because emblems are so culturally specific, it would be impossible to list them all.

Immediately upon entering a new country, Marines and security personnel should quickly determine what the local emblems are. The psychologist Paul Ekman studied several cultures and identified emblematic gestures that indicate "greeting and departing, replying, direction/locomotion, insulting or evaluating another's actions or appearance, referring to a person's physical state, or announcing a person's current condition or state."[93] With limitations in interpreter/translator support in foreign countries, understanding these culturally specific emblems can ensure all Marines on patrol know how to give basic commands that the *local population* understands and make rudimentary assessments about conversations and relationships when they cannot understand the words.

Kinesic Baselines and Anomalies

As we've discussed earlier, it is important to constantly establish a baseline for the area we occupy. This can be done at the macro level using all the domains but can also be done for each individual domain. We want to establish a baseline for a person's body language so we have a starting point for follow-up observations and can identify changes that occur. A kinesic baseline is simply the cluster you use to characterize a person as (dominant, submissive, uncomfortable, or comfortable). When the situation and time allows, a combat profiler can add into that initial classification with the interested vs. uninterested cluster to provide a more detailed picture.

The reason we use a cluster as the baseline is because this can be established *before* you approach someone. Often, a visible sign of authority will cause a change in people's behavior. Picture a situation in which a police officer is approaching a group of teenagers in the mall. Before the police officer approaches, an observer would probably note much dominant behavior in the teens when they think they haven't done anything wrong and are comfortable with their friends. However, when they see the police officer approach, you would likely see a shift in the group as some would become uncomfortable with the police officer, some might become submissive, and some may attempt to become more dominant at the presence of authority. Without establishing that initial baseline before he approached, the officer wouldn't be able to notice those changes. While a group of teenagers might not pose a significant threat, those changes become immediately more important for Marines on patrol overseas or a police officer on patrol in a gang-controlled neighborhood. Those changes could be the first indicator that the gang member has decided he doesn't want to return to jail and would rather take his chances by fighting or shooting his way out of the situation. Being proactive might only be a few seconds left of bang, but those few seconds and those initial changes in behavior can be the difference between success and failure on the battlefield.

Kinesic Anomalies

Up to this point, we have provided a means of establishing a baseline, but the goal is for combat profilers to quickly observe anomalies in order to proactively identify threats. As we discussed, an anomaly is anything that rises above or falls below our baseline. Regarding kinesics, an anomaly can be any behavior that does not fit the situation: someone uncomfortable in a casual setting, a person who is overly interested, or behavior that seems overly dominant or too submissive. Besides these types of anomalies, there are several specific anomalies combat profilers should look for: threat behaviors, kinesic slips, smuggling behavior, and "acting" natural.

Specific Anomalies That Require Action

Identifying threat behavior is discussed last because it seems to go against most of what we have talked about up to this point, especially the Rule of Three for establishing a cluster. However, as we discussed above, combat profilers don't always need to observe three indicators before making a decision. In some cases, only one indicator is needed to take action. Military personnel and law enforcement officers have the legal responsibility and the authority to take action whenever a person poses an immediate threat to them or others. It is the driving concept that created rules of engagement—we exist to protect. There are certain behaviors in the category of threat behavior that do not require a cluster to be built; whenever they are identified, they require immediate attention. Police officers are trained early on to identify many of these behaviors and have consistently mentioned them when discussing threats.

The first area of the body Marines should observe on a person is the hands. Checking the hands of a person ensures that the person is not holding a weapon and is not preparing to strike. Marines should ensure that any person they come into contact with exposes his or her hands—this will help to ensure the person is not an immediate threat. Making the decision to contact a person often involves getting physically close and creates a significant amount of risk: limited reaction time, increased number of options for the attacker to do harm, and less skill required by an attacker to do harm.

Additionally, hands can often times betray where a person's attention is. If a person has something concealed they don't want discovered, such as a gun, a knife, drugs, stolen items, etc., that person will often touch or pat that area on the body where the object is concealed, as if to ensure the object has not been lost and it is still hidden from view. Repeated patting can indicate that the person has a weapon or something else worth identifying concealed on his or her body.

Another indicator to look for is people who are "checking their six." This is when a person looks over the shoulder to see who is around or behind them. Only people who are aware of their surroundings conduct this behavior, and since most people do not bother to search for threats or bother to be aware of their surroundings, this is an indicator that demands further observation. As discussed earlier, people are categorized into one of three categories: good guys, bad guys, and the rest of the population. Good guys (Marines, soldiers, police officers, etc.) are trained to be aware of their surroundings and will conduct this act of checking their six to see if anyone is approaching them, to look at the people around them, and to maintain a general level of awareness. Bad guys (criminals, insurgents, terrorists, etc.) will conduct the same type of behavior to assess their area for easy targets and to ensure there are no "good guys" around them who could catch them in the act. Any person checking his or her "six" is immediately an anomaly and deserves further observation. A decision is definitely required in these situations, even if just further observation to identify the person's intentions.

Kinesic Slips

A kinesic slip occurs when a person's nonverbal behavior betrays the person's words. Nonverbal communication should complement and supplement verbal communication, either adding emphasis or illustrating a point, but can also contradict the words used. So when the nonverbal communication contradicts the words used to communicate the same point, combat profilers should be alerted that something might be awry. For instance, if a person is recalling a situation and says that he was driving down a road and turned left at the intersection while his hands pointed to the right, more credence should be given to the gesture. This is because the gesture occurred without any thought or control; however, the story may have been consciously altered to fit a particular purpose, that is, a lie. If a person is being questioned about whether "bad guys" are in the area (e.g., insurgents, criminals) and says "no" but nods "yes," then weight should be given to the gesture, not the words. The person is subconsciously and nonverbally telling the truth (i.e., bad guys are in the area) but they are verbally lying or concealing information.

Smuggling Behavior

Picture a person attempting to smuggle drugs through an airport, or a person attempting to smuggle a weapon onto a plane. What behaviors would this person display? First, situations like this pose significant risks for the person attempting to smuggle something past security. Particularly in places such as airports, there is a high possibility that the smuggler will be caught. Anytime there is a high chance that a person will be caught doing something, that person will experience some type of distress. Furthermore, the person's body language will provide indicators of distress and discomfort. Uncomfortable behaviors might be displayed. Additionally, the person's body will display visible physiological effects of the stress. Second, smugglers have a high degree of concern for whatever it is they are smuggling. Unless they have trained extensively to pay no attention to the object they are smuggling and are absolutely confident that they still have it in their possession, smugglers will devote some effort and attention toward the object. An individual smuggling a weapon or drugs on his body will occasionally (or sometimes often) reach for the object and touch it to ensure its safety. Normal individuals do this with things such as car keys, wallets, and cell phones. When people get up and move, they often pat their pocket to ensure they still have their wallet, watch, and cell phone—these are important to them and they don't want to lose them. Smugglers do the same thing. Why do we discuss smugglers here? The behavior that smugglers exhibit is the same type of behavior that suicide bombers, or someone carrying a weapon into a place they are not supposed to, will exhibit.

"Acting" Natural

One of the principles of human nature that combat profiling is based upon is that people only look natural when they are naturally doing something. Briefly, this means that, when we are truly focused on some activity, our actions will be smooth and fluid, and we will appear like we are concentrating on the activity in which we are engaged. However, if we are only "going through the motions" of the activity, but are instead mentally doing something else (e.g., thinking or worrying about something else, trying to observe others, etc.), then our body language will give us away. We will appear unfocused, will move slower or faster than we should, will over-exaggerate or under-exaggerate our motions, and will not move fluidly or smoothly. Consider the behavior of a construction worker laying bricks at a construction site across from the White House. Now, if this construction worker is truly concentrating on his job, all of his mental and physical energy will be focused on the task at hand: mixing mortar, moving bricks, digging, etc. He will most likely not be concerned with what is going on around him and will be moving at a speed appropriate to his activity.

Now imagine this same construction worker attempting to look like he is laying bricks but is, instead, conducting surveillance on the White House. Since no one can really multitask—i.e., truly do two things at once—this individual will have to divide his attention. He will have to shift back and forth between the job he is acting like he is doing and his primary task of collecting information. He will move slower than he should overall, or he may try to act quicker than normal during the times he is "working" to make up for the time lost while observing. He will certainly appear unfocused; in fact, he may become so concerned with the task of observing the White House that he may completely lose all situational awareness and forget he is supposed to be laying bricks.

Why do we bring up this example? Farmers in Afghanistan who are actually collecting information on U.S. patrols or criminals conducting observation on potential targets while acting like they are doing something else will exhibit the same type of behavior as our construction worker above.

Kinesics Summary

Before a person takes any action or makes any gesture, the decision is first made in his brain, either consciously or subconsciously. When that decision is made, people will begin to prepare their bodies for that act and will begin to telegraph their intentions and let others know what they are *about* to do. Time spent developing the ability to read and understand body language, both quickly and accurately, will provide much insight into other people's intentions and emotions.

Kinesics Takeaways

1. One gesture is insufficient to make an observation; always form a cluster of three indicators leading to the same conclusion.

2. Clusters should be formed using indicators from below the shoulders to prevent misinterpreting facial expressions.

3. Search for body language that is the result of the limbic system's freeze, flight, or fight response to stress and the perception of threats.

4. Dominant cluster: The fight response is defined by the behavior people show when attempting to make themselves appear larger.

5. Submissive cluster: The absence of the fight response is defined by the behavior people show when attempting to make themselves appear smaller.

6. Uncomfortable cluster: The flight response is defined by the behavior people show when they are displaying distancing or blocking behavior to protect themselves.

7. Comfortable cluster: No threat perceived; this is defined by behavior that shows openness.

8. Interested vs. uninterested cluster: Where a person's attention is focused.

9. Threat indicators: Include smuggling behavior (patting an area on the body), situational awareness (checking their six) and attempting to act natural.

4. BIOMETRICS

There are, of course, many surface manifestations of excitement. The contraction of blood vessels with resulting pallor, the pouring out of "cold sweat," the stopping of saliva-flow so that the "tongue cleaves to the roof of the mouth," the dilation of the pupils, the rising of the hairs, the rapid beating of the heart, the hurried respiration, the trembling and twitching of the muscles, especially those about the lips—all these bodily changes are well recognized accompaniments of pain and great emotional disturbance, such as fear, horror, and deep disgust. But these disturbances of the even routine of life, which have been commonly noted, are mainly superficial and therefore readily observable. Even the increased rapidity of the heartbeat is noted at the surface in the pulsing of the arteries. *

When a person experiences some type of stress, a threatening situation, or a strong emotional response, that person's body experiences certain physiological changes—mostly caused by the response of the autonomic nervous system (ANS) and by the release of certain hormones such as adrenaline. In fact, these autonomic changes provide the foundation for polygraph tests.[94] These uncontrollable, automatic, and observable reactions that people experience are called biometric cues. Because these cues are closely related to the fight-or-flight response, combat profilers can observe and read people's biometric cues as indicators that a person may be a potential threat.

Why are biometrics important? In short, biometric cues are caused by emotional changes. People experience emotions when something is happening or is about to happen (even just thinking something will occur) that will affect their

---

*Walter Cannon, *Bodily Changes in Pain, Hunger, Fear and Rage,* 1915.

well-being. Emotions prepare a person to react quickly to a situation by causing physiological changes that help deal with what caused the emotion.[95] While these emotions can be positive or negative, combat profilers are concerned with negative emotions such as anger, fear, and contempt and the way that the fight-or-flight response can be observed on the body as opposed to the facial expressions associated with the emotions.

Biometric Baselines and Anomalies

The body generally tries to maintain equilibrium, which is a normal state of being in functions such as heart rate, respiration rate, body temperature, and blood pressure. When conditions change, the body reacts to them and attempts to adapt to the new conditions. That state of equilibrium and balance will become the baseline when it comes to biometric cues, and the observable changes will become the initial indicators of an anomaly.

When establishing baselines with regard to any domain, combat profilers need to understand the context of the situation. This will determine what is normal and what is anomalous. For instance, a person shivering may be an anomaly—shivering is an indicator that the autonomic nervous system has withdrawn the blood from the extremities and diverted it to the major organs and muscle groups in preparation for a fight-or-flight response.[96] This could also indicate that the individual may be anxious, afraid, or even angry, but could also be a response to the person simply being cold. It is important to identify if the person is shivering because of the environment,[97] rather than some physiological effect of emotions. Therefore, the first question combat profilers must ask when identifying an anomaly is: Does this person's behavior fit the situation? Once the baseline has been established, anomalies can more easily be detected. There are three main types of anomalies with regard to biometrics:

1. An individual whose biometric cues do not fit the situation.

2. A change in the observed biometric cues, whether sudden or gradual, though a sudden change communicates a more immediate change in the person's emotions, which would be a more urgent indicator.

3. Indicators that an individual is attempting to mask or hide potential biometric cues, or someone giving off nonverbal indicators of attempting to control them through pacifying behaviors.

Emotions and Their Biometric Cues

ANGER

As Paul Ekman says, "the face of attack, of violence, is anger."[98] Anger may be caused by being or feeling physically or psychologically restrained, insulted or harmed, taken advantage of, or many other reasons.[99] From an evolutionary perspective, anger was an important emotion for survival since it helped to mobilize an individual to fight a threat.[100] Anger is the most common dangerous emotion since the motive of anger often is to harm the target.[101] When a person experiences anger, that person's body gives off certain honest signals that communicate to others that the person is angry. An angry person may flare their nostrils and become red in the face.[102] Anger is associated with increased heart rate, increased respiratory activity (faster breathing),[103] and facial flushing.[104]

Fear

Fear is an emotion that is closely related to anger.[105] Fear is caused by events or situations that signal danger[106] as well as the threat of physical or psychological harm.[107] Evolution has predisposed humans to a few main responses to a threat discussed earlier—freeze, flight, or fight. Fear is associated with the flight and freeze responses, though anger may quickly follow fear, which may lead to a fight response, particularly if it seems as though fleeing or freezing will not work.[108] Fear may also differ depending on the situation, whether the threat is occurring right now or if it will occur in the future. An immediate threat leads to action (flight/freeze) to respond to the threat. An impending threat leads to increased vigilance.[109] Just as with anger, there are visible and non-visible physiological reactions by the body. Fear is associated with increased heart rate, vasoconstriction (paling of the skin), and faster breathing.[110] Pupil dilation, sweating, and increased blood flow are also associated with fear.[111] Anxiety, which is related to fear, may cause pupil constriction and faster or shallower than normal breathing.[112]

Contempt

The two emotions discussed above, anger and fear, are directly related to the body's fight-or-flight mechanism. Contempt, although not directly related to fight-or-flight, often includes an element of anger and can easily lead to a person becoming angry toward the target of contempt, which then may lead to violence. Disgust, which is closely related to contempt, corresponds to faster breathing and accelerated heart rate[113] as well as increased salivation.[114]

Our body gives off signals that it is experiencing these emotions, and because these emotions are often spontaneous, the signals are often spontaneous. Some physiological aspects that are associated with emotional change include blood pressure, heart rate, respiration, salivary secretion, sweating, muscle tension, tremors, and eye blinking.[115] Furthermore, when someone does realize that they are experiencing these emotions, they may attempt to conceal, repress, or mask them—which may be, at times, an even more obvious indicator that something is going on. It is the job of the combat profiler to pick up on these indicators. The next several sections will introduce specific indicators.

Eyes

It has often been said that the eyes are a window into a person's soul. While this may or may not be true, the eyes do tell a lot about a person's emotions. The eyes respond immediately to stress and provide obvious indicators that a person is undergoing some type of stress. There are three main biometric cues that relate to the eyes: pupil dilation/constriction, blinking, and tunnel vision.

Pupil Dilation and Constriction

A person's pupil is normally between 2 mm to 5 mm in diameter, but can contract to 1.5 mm and can dilate up to 9 mm. It can also react to stimuli in 0.2 seconds,[116] which means that the pupils can provide an immediate indicator of a person's emotions. The late psychologist and University of Chicago professor Eckhard H. Hess conducted numerous studies demonstrating that pupil size can be a reliable indicator of attitude and emotions—when people see things they think are positive or pleasurable, their pupils dilate, but when they see things they think are negative or that cause anxiety, their pupils constrict.[117] Pupil dilation has often been shown to be associated with both anger and fear.[118] Pupils also dilate due to new or interesting stimuli, when a person is focused and paying attention to something, when concentrating, or when experiencing pain. The pupil sometimes constricts in response to negative stimuli, as also demonstrated by Hess. For a combat profiler, any significant change in a person's pupil size should be taken as an indicator that something has aroused that individual, whether positively or negatively, and that person has experienced some type of emotion.

BLINKING

Blinking is such a common and routine activity that it is often forgotten. A normal person blinks thousands of times each day and rarely notices it; however, blinking is an incredibly reliable indicator that a person is undergoing stress. For instance, in 1999, former President Clinton was under significant stress during the deposition concerning his relationship with Monica Lewinsky. His body language and speech clearly confirmed this. In addition to more obvious behavioral and verbal signs, Clinton's blinking also indicated that he was extremely uncomfortable and upset. During the deposition, Solomon Wisenberg asked Clinton a series of fairly explicit questions regarding his relationship with Lewinsky. Take any one-minute segment of this conversation, and Clinton's average blink rate is about sixty blinks per minute. Contrast this with his blink rate during a speech he gave in January 1998, in which he initially responds to the allegations regarding Lewinsky. During this speech, Clinton does not appear to be under much stress, and his blink rate is between twelve to fifteen blinks per minute. His blink rate while under stress was about four times his blink rate while not under stress. A person's normal blink rate is between six to ten times per minute, but blinking increases when a person is under stress,[119] emotionally aroused,[120] or when a person attempts to mask emotions.[121]

Blink rate can also be an indicator that someone is extremely focused since blinking has been shown to decrease when one is under significant cognitive load or highly focused.[122] Attempting to suppress an emotion is physiologically taxing, and a specific indicator of someone attempting to suppress an emotion is increased blinking. Based on this information, combat profilers should consider significant blinking as an indicator that someone is experiencing a high level of stress (and may be anxious, scared, or nervous), and very little blinking as an indicator that someone is extremely focused—perhaps mission focused.

TUNNEL VISION AND MISSION FOCUS

The area of a person's focused vision is relatively small, and peripheral vision is critical to understand one's surroundings and allowing the brain to make sense of the world. However, when a person's peripheral vision is lost and focused vision is reduced, that person can have significant difficulty doing even the simplest tasks. Tunnel vision is the extreme loss of peripheral vision. It is an autonomic response that happens as the result of severe stress and an excessive heart rate.[123] When a person has tunnel vision, that person will appear to not be paying attention to the surrounding environment (which is true) and will easily run into objects that would have normally been noticed and avoided. Combat profilers will not actually see the loss of peripheral vision occur, but they will see the effects of the loss of peripheral vision.[124]

"Face Your Enemy"

The face reveals much about a person's emotions, more than most people understand and appreciate. In addition to expressing emotions, the face also gives off certain biometric cues that combat profilers can observe to help identify anomalies. The main indicators on the face are facial flushing (blushing), paling/blanching, and dry mouth.

Facial Flushing (Blushing) and Paling

Reddening of the face, that is, facial flushing, is caused by the capillaries in the face dilating and being filled with blood (vasodilations) and can be the result of several situations. For instance, a person's face may redden during or after intense physical activity, such as exercise. However, facial flushing also occurs when an individual is angry and intending to fight.[125] This reddening may also spread to a person's neck. In contrast, paling is associated with fear and anxiety as the body takes blood away from the skin and extremities (vasoconstriction) and diverts it to the important muscle groups.[126] Paling may also occur with forms of anger associated with bracing or protecting one's self against an attack.[127] The key is that any significant color change in a person's face is a clear indicator that the person is experiencing a significant emotional response.

Dry Mouth

Dry mouth is often associated with increased activity of the autonomic nervous system. It would seem that the autonomic nervous system diverts needed fluids to more important parts of the body and functions, such as sweating. Increased emotional arousal has also been shown to increase swallowing.[128] In fact, increased swallowing is also associated with the repression of emotions, particularly embarrassment. As one researcher writes, "This fairly easily observed behavior (i.e., swallowing) might be a useful cue to observers that someone is experiencing an emotional state but trying to not show it."[129]

Chest and Torso

Emotional responses often affect the entire body, not just the face. The torso and limbs may also provide indicators that are important for combat profilers to observe. Two of the major indicators are rapid breathing and shaking. Increased respiration (i.e., faster breathing) and irregular respiration are associated with negative emotions (e.g., anger and fear).[130] Another indicator related to the chest and torso is shivering, which results when the autonomic nervous system diverts blood from the periphery (hands, skin, etc.) and sends it to the major muscles—individuals who experience this may feel cold and begin to shiver. This can happen during both fight and flight responses. Because of feeling cold, a person may display particular nonverbal indicators, such as crossing the arms across the chest or rubbing the arms and chest to warm up.

Indicators associated with the limbs include shaking, sweaty palms, otherwise excessive movement (fidgeting), and loss of fine motor skills. Trembling may occur after physical activity because of extreme vasoconstriction in the extremities or as a result of the release of adrenaline.[131] In fact, adrenaline increases heart rate and causes the constriction of blood vessels in addition to trembling.[132] When a person's heart rate exceeds 115 beats per minute (bpm), fine motor skills begin to deteriorate. After 145 bpm, complex motor skills begin to be lost.[133] When our autonomic nervous system is aroused, one of the results is an increase in motor activity, and even when one attempts to suppress this energy, it may still appear as small fidgets and other "nervous" behavior. These fidgets are honest signals of increased autonomic nervous system activity.[134]

Masking, Hiding, Comforting

Although most people do not consciously know how the ANS and limbic system react during times of emotional stress, they still learn how to deal with the effects. Every person displays types of pacifying behaviors, which may be indicators that they are experiencing the types of autonomic-biological effects discussed in this chapter. Although they were discussed in detail in the kinesics chapter, we want to briefly touch on them here since they are indicators that someone is either trying to mask or respond to these biometric cues. For instance, watch a poker tournament, and you will notice that some individuals wear sunglasses during the poker game. They do not wear sunglasses because it is bright inside, but because they understand that their pupils could potentially give away their emotional response to the cards they have in their hand. Taking this a step further, in combat situations, we want to be suspicious of individuals whose clothes do not fit the environment, who wear too many clothes, or whose clothes are too loose. Each of these may be indicators that the person is attempting to mask biometric cues their body gives off when they experience stress. Nonverbally, pacifying behaviors consist of rubbing the neck, breathing deeply and slowly, rubbing the arms and chest, or rubbing the legs when seated. These actions are done to relax hair follicles, slow down respiration, inhibit shaking and shivering, and generally calm oneself down. For example, as a person experiences increased respiration as the person's body attempts to take in more oxygen, the person may attempt to control his or her breathing by taking long, slow breaths.

Using Biometrics to the
Combat Profiler's Advantage

Biometric cues provide immediate and accurate indicators of the type of emotion that a person is experiencing, as well as indicators of sudden emotional changes. However, identifying biometric cues requires being close enough to one's target of observation to be able to identify small changes such as pupil dilation, reddening or paling of the skin, and sweating. Some indicators can be seen from further away, such as rapid breathing. By looking for these biometric cues, combat profilers can read the emotions of those around them and identify those individuals who are experiencing some type of emotional stress or change in emotion. Someone attempting to smuggle or steal, discreetly escape, harm someone, or do anything in which they may experience some type of strong negative emotion will display one or more of these indicators. Since rarely does only one indicator appear by itself, combat profilers will usually be able to identify other anomalies, from either this or another domain, to confirm that what the profiler had observed biometrically was an accurate indicator. The next section will build on this knowledge of human nonverbal comunication and provide further indicators to identify potential threats.

Biometric Cues Takeaways

1. Biometric cues are the uncontrollable and automatic responses to stress.
2. Biometric cues contribute to the clusters of individual behavior.
3. Reddening occurs as the result of anger or embarrassment and is seen on the face, neck or extremities.

4. Paling occurs during fear and is seen by the absence of normal skin color as blood is pulled away from the extremities.
5. Pupils dilate when something pleasurable or positive is seen as well as in times of fear.
6. Pupils constrict when something negative is observed.
7. Blink rate increases during times of stress.
8. Dry mouth occurs as moisture is drawn from extremities and can be observed by a person licking his or her lips.

5. PROXEMICS

proximate, *adj.*, *1. next or nearest in space, order, time, etc.*
proximity, *n.*, *1. the state or quality of being near.*

"Making correct inferences about the imminent behavior of others has adaptive benefits, and misunderstanding what another individual intends to do can seriously impair survival."[135]

The way humans use space to communicate is called proxemics. Like other animals, humans move toward what they are attracted to and move away from what they fear. For the combat profiler, the two most significant factors with regard to proxemics are relationship and status. Relationship affects the distance at which two people will stand. For instance, friends stand closer to one another than they do with strangers. Status is significant in how people use space to communicate, as subordinates rarely initiate contact with someone of higher social rank. Understanding relationship and status in a given situation is critical to making good observations. Two friends who are maintaining a significant separation from one another may be an anomaly, just as a subordinate initiating contact with a person of higher status may be an anomaly.

The use of proxemics in combat profiling rests on several key principles:

1. People are drawn toward things they like, that they are attracted to, that make them feel safe and comfortable. People avoid and move way from things they dislike, are afraid of, or that make them feel unsafe and uncomfortable.[136]

2. The closer people choose to be, generally the more comfortable those people are with one another.

3. People who know each other will stand near each other. In any crowd, people who know each other will be next to each other, and those people who know each other best will be the closest to each other.

Proxemics makes it possible for Marines to identify potential threats by observing how others use space. Proxemics involves two main elements: distance, as it reveals relationships or attitudes, and movement, as an indicator of intention.

Distance

Proxemics provides combat profilers with the ability to evaluate groups of people and determine significant aspects of the relationships between them and their attitudes toward one another. The group's relationships in space provide the observer with a wealth of information about each individual in the group as well as the group as a whole.

Anthropologist Edward T. Hall has defined four proxemic zones. These zones are the general distances that people maintain from one another, depending upon their level of comfort with one another. Although specific distances are culturally dependent, the four zones are still valid ways of using the distance between people to make a determination about their relationships. Hall's four zones are the intimate, the personal, the social, and the public.

1. THE INTIMATE ZONE

The intimate zone is the area that is closest to the body. It is the space normally reserved only for people in the closest of relationships.[137] Spouses, boyfriends and girlfriends, children, parents, and very close friends are usually the only people willingly permitted into this area. This area is well within arm's reach and provides the most risk for someone to do harm. This is the reason people are selective about who is granted access into this space.

At times, the intimate zone boundary is crossed without consent. There are many reasons that this could occur. One of these reasons could be because one person is attempting to establish dominance over another. Since a proxemic violation "occurs when some actual harm is done by the invasion,"[138] the person violating the proxemic boundary may be trying to make the other person feel uncomfortable and ultimately submissive to either gain or maintain influence. These times when people are forced into socially "close" situations will cause a limbic system response, as the body prepares to deal with the threat. A person whose intimate zone has been violated and who feels defensive or uncomfortable may put up barriers or display pacifying behaviors (kinesics), begin to blush (biometrics), or move away from the person to re-establish proper separation (proxemics).

There are situations in which violations of the intimate zone become unavoidable, such as on crowded city streets, in airplanes, elevators, or in professional environments like a doctor's office, a beauty parlor, or a barbershop. People are generally acutely aware of invasions, not only because they don't want others intruding on their space, but also because they don't want to violate the space of others.[139] In such situations, there is an expectation that others will make an effort to maintain the proper distance. When that is not the case, the limbic system recognizes a potential threat and responds accordingly.

2. The Personal Zone

The personal zone is the second smallest circle surrounding a person. It is the space within which most friends and acquaintances interact.[140] This distance is generally about arm's length and is the conversational separation at which most daily interaction is conducted. People who operate in this zone generally have some relationship but are not close enough to allow each other into the intimate zone.

As with the intimate zone, situations arise in which individuals are forced into one another's personal zone, such as in shopping malls, restaurants, or public transportation. The kinesic cluster of interested vs. uninterested will provide confirmation that this boundary has been violated. Signs that two people are comfortable within each other's personal zones may be an acknowledgement between them such as eye contact, nods, feet or torso turning toward the person, or handshakes. If no indicators of a positive relationship exist, this could indicate that the two are intentionally trying to avoid each other.

3. Social and Public Zones

The social and public zones are the two largest zones. These are the distances at which people prefer to keep strangers.[141] The two zones are addressed jointly in this section because both indicate the same relationship: no relationship. Why do people tend to keep strangers at a distance? Safety. As distance increases, the options available to an attacker decrease.

For the purposes of combat profiling, the social and public zones are beyond arm's length.

How people interact with the space around and between them is a significant dynamic and predictor of human behavior anywhere in the world. Proxemic distance can indicate the nature of relationships between people of a group and relationships between groups. Identifying the proxemic zones between people does not require that the observer be up close and personal. Observation can be done with standoff (i.e., sufficient distance to protect oneself) using binoculars or other optics. This observation is one that the combat profiler must study and master. The objective, remember, is to place ourselves and those we are protecting "left of bang."

A note about cultural differences: The exact distance of the four zones described above varies from culture to culture. On a recent trip to Tokyo, a Japanese male and an American Marine were observed in conversation. The Japanese man continually tried to move closer to the Marine to establish the conversational distance customary in Japanese culture. Each time he did so, the Marine backed away, seeking the comfort (to him) of the normal American conversational distance. This "proxemic dance" continued throughout the encounter.

Movement

If distance is the first element of proxemics, movement is the second.

People move for a purpose, and the way a person moves can reveal that person's intentions. A predator creeping in for the kill looks different than a person casually searching for a friend, and an attacker with violent intentions moving quickly toward his or her target looks different than a person rapidly approaching a friend with excitement. The ability to determine intentions from motion is a skill evolved by humans over millions of years. As one study states, "One of our most fundamental cognitive adaptations is the ability to infer the intentions of others."[142]

Combat profilers classify movement into three categories: movement toward, movement away, and idle movement.

Movement toward can be both positive and negative; it can mean friendly or hostile intent. Movement away can mean evasion or flight, or simply movement away from one thing toward another without any negative intention. Idle movement can include activities such as waiting or other benign purposes, but can also communicate surveillance. Combat profilers must distinguish between these types of movement. The best way to learn is practice: to place ourselves in scenarios where we can observe different intentional movements and develop file folders on each type.

Imagine you are walking along a busy street. People are passing in every direction. Most are paying no attention to you. No one is increasing or decreasing his speed relative to yours, and no one is changing his direction. You can quickly rule out that anyone ahead of you is attempting to evade you. You observe those individuals who are facing you and walking toward you. Again, no one seems to notice you. No one increases or decreases his speed. Their angles relative to you remain the same. The few people who are walking close to your path do change their direction a bit to avoid you. You can quickly infer that none of these people is a threat. However, as you glance to your rear, you notice one individual who does seem to be increasing his speed and whose angle and direction matches yours. As you turn down a side street, he turns the same way. You increase your speed. He matches it. You cross the road. When you turn back, you see that this individual has changed his angle and direction to take the shortest route to your location, and he is now in a dead sprint. Apart from his facial expressions or other body language, you can quickly infer that he is chasing you. You must now determine if the person following you is a threat; kinesics and biometrics help you to do so.

Proxemic Pushes and Pulls

A foundational dynamic of human nature is that people will approach things they like and which they expect will deliver pleasure and avoid things that are unappealing or could cause them pain.[143]

In combat profiling, movement toward a person or thing is called a proxemic pull. The opposite, movement away, is a proxemic push.

1. PROXEMIC PULL

A proxemic pull occurs when a person or group is drawn to another person, group, object, or place. Proxemic pulls occur for many reasons: because the person being pulled is interested; because the other person, object, or place can fulfill a need; a relationship or association exists; or there is a degree of attraction and curiosity. Proxemic pulls occur when someone does not perceive any threat, so the body is not prepared for fight or flight. Proxemic pulls are significant to combat profilers because they focus the profiler's attention on specific interactions that provide insight into the group being observed.

Proxemic pulls are indicators that some person or element stands out from the baseline. If people are attracted and drawn to a person, combat profilers should either continue to observe that person or contact that individual to figure out what makes that person significant. Consider a drug dealer operating on a street. This individual will be continually approached by others and will have a high degree of situational awareness. His interactions will exhibit significant hand-to-hand contact, which is the obvious sign of possible drug deals. Although the hand-to-hand contact is the indicator of illegal activity, it is the proxemic pull that will initially draw the combat or law enforcement profiler's attention.

Marines deployed overseas deal with this dynamic every day. On many patrols, Marines will designate one member as the "candy man." The candy man is the Marine with the backpack full of sweets, pens, pencils, and anything else to give to the local kids. As soon as the candy man has been discovered by the local children, other youngsters are proxemically pulled to that one Marine. While the candy-man pull can be a benefit for Marines as they strive to build relationships with the locals so they can root out the enemy, the enemy often uses these proxemic pulls to their advantage as well by staging attacks as people congregate.

2. NEGATIVE PROXEMIC PULL

Suicide bombers seek centers of proxemic pull: a market, a house of worship, a medical support mission. They go where the highest number of people are.

A stark proxemic reality is that less-skilled attackers need to get close to us to harm us. This makes it critical for profilers to recognize when proxemic pulls are occurring and to be alert for these potential threats.

Insurgents also attempt to use proxemic pulls as a means to bait Americans into areas where they may be attacked. Insurgents don't have an endless supply of equipment, munitions, or manpower. They must be more efficient in *where* they choose to strike. They can do this in one of two ways—either by studying our tactics, habits, and patterns to predict where we *might* be in the future or by doing something to draw American forces into an area where they, the enemy, are waiting. Insurgents might use several tactics to create a proxemic pull: cause a civil disturbance to force stand-by forces to deploy, emplace a decoy IED to force explosive specialists to respond, open fire on a patrol, then flee to cause the patrol to give chase. By understanding the enemy's method of proxemic pulls, patrol leaders can use tactical cunning to think through *where* the enemy is trying to pull the patrol and outmaneuver the enemy instead of getting ambushed.

3. PROXEMIC PUSH

A proxemic push is the opposite of a proxemic pull; it is the movement away from another person, place, or object. A proxemic push occurs to avoid a real or potential threat or because of fear or uncertainty created by a lack of knowledge. In contrast to the proxemic pull, there is usually a "flight" element to the decision to move away from a perceived threat.

In civilian society, individuals rarely find themselves in situations that require immediate physical flight. That doesn't mean that proxemic pushes don't happen every day. The businessman being criticized by his superior during a committee meeting may roll his chair backwards a few inches and then lean even farther away to create as much separation from his boss as possible without making the discomfort obvious. The need to separate oneself from a threat is universal. The combat profiler can and must be aware of this.

Patrols by U.S. forces in foreign nations, such as Afghanistan, have a tendency to pull children toward them. However, at times, a U.S. force may encounter situations in which children or other locals purposefully avoid patrols. Do the locals have advanced warning of an impending ambush? Have the locals been threatened by insurgents with consequences if they interact with or help the American forces? In these situations, an American patrol has caused a proxemic push. Children and other locals are repelled for reasons of their own survival.

Good guys and bad guys are continually engaging in a proxemic push and pull dance. As always, the combat profiler must establish the baseline and then immediately hunt for anomalies. In proxemics, these anomalies are defined by two distinct factors: distance and movement.

Imagine your patrol has entered a village. Your squad car drives into a neighborhood. The first anomaly that should alert a profiler is a sudden change in proxemic behavior, especially avoidance (proxemic push). When people suddenly grant greater proxemic space than is normal, it is likely that they have been pushed away from something to ensure their own safety and survival. The second anomaly is decreased proxemic standoff. Have individuals placed themselves closer (anomaly) than they should be (baseline)? Are they moving even closer? Is that movement accelerating?

The domain of proxemics is about identifying and confirming people's relationships and intentions based on how they interact with the space around them. These fundamentals of proxemics can be applied anywhere in the world. While the physical distances will change for the different proxemic zones, the zones will still imply the same information about the relationships that people have with each other.

Just like the other domains discussed up to this point, the proxemic zones and proxemic pushes and pulls are observations that people have been making their entire lives. The only difference is that combat profiling is now classifying and defining behavior, which allows for more intelligent decisions that can be communicated to other people to explain the human behavior being observed.

Key Takeaways—Proxemics

1. Proxemics is the interpretation of space between people and other people or objects.

2. Intimate zone: Reserved for only the closest of relationships, inside one arm's-length distance.

3. Personal zone: Reserved for friends and acquaintances, generally about one arm's distance.

4. Social and Public zones: Distance where strangers are maintained.

5. Proxemic pull: The physical movements toward a person or object, likely caused by things that are considered attractive, safe, and positive.

6. Proxemic push: The physical movement away from a person or object, likely caused by things that are considered harmful, unappealing, and negative.

6. GEOGRAPHICS

What Are Geographics?

"In Los Angeles, every street is claimed by one gang or another. It doesn't matter if it is in the suburbs or the street the police station is on, a gang will claim they own it. Some streets are more contested than others, but the first step in understanding crime here is to understand who has claimed what."
—Los Angeles police officer, Gang Task Force

The first principle of Geographics is that human beings (and animals as well) act with greater confidence in areas with which they are familiar. Home field advantage is real. Individuals move fluidly, comfortably, and confidently in areas they feel at home in, but more deliberately, slowly, and with greater caution in areas where they don't know "the lay of the land." Crime and insurgent activity occurs almost always in settings where the criminal and the insurgent have established a high degree of fluency and familiarity. Because of this, Marines and law enforcement professionals need to be capable of identifying individuals and groups who have developed an intuitive understanding of their environment. This begins by studying how people move through the neighborhoods and villages with which they are familiar.

Who is the enemy?

Where is he?

As you, the combat profiler, seek the foe hiding in plain sight and in plain clothes, the domain of geographics is indispensable. Geographics allows you to make assessments about the relationship between the people and the village, the neighborhood, and the land. Geographics provides a methodology for breaking down the area of operations into manageable sections: areas in which the enemy conducts attacks, areas in which he lives or is based, and paths and byways by which he moves from one location to another. Just as the skilled hunter knows his prey's tracks and trails, dens and sleeping sites, so we combat profilers must learn not just the enemy, but the ground he moves upon, takes shelter in, and from which he strikes.

1. NATURAL LINES OF DRIFT

If you have ever seen the movie *Ferris Bueller's Day Off*, consider the scene where Ferris is in a race to beat his mom back home so that he won't get caught ditching school. Ferris knew the beeline route. He knew which fences to jump and which backyards to cut through. He knew the way home as intimately as insurgents crossing from Pakistan to Afghanistan know the "ratlines" through the mountains. He knew the natural lines of drift (NLDs).

The combat profiler must know these lines too. To identify where the enemy will be, we must learn how he intends to get there.

In any environment, humans and animals will seek the path of least resistance. In anthropological terms, movement is costly, and in order for most types of movement to be worthwhile, getting to the goal should not cost more in time, energy, safety, etc. than it is worth to get there. When traveling from one place to another, people take paths that are simple, safe, and obstacle-free. Note: This is not always the shortest way. Additionally, every environment is shaped in ways that provide certain natural paths for people to follow. This is as true in urban environments as it is in rural environments. The combination of these factors—simple, safe, and obstacle-free paths that follow the natural outlay of an area—create NLDs. Once the combat profiler begins to look for these pathways, he starts seeing them everywhere. NLDs may be paths worn through mulched plant beds in mall parking lots, game trails through the woods, or openings in fences.

Combat profilers can use NLDs to predict where and how the enemy will travel. Identifying NLDs is critical because these are the paths the enemy often takes to move between his base of operations and the places he conducts attacks. Marines normally consider NLDs when thinking tactically. Patrol leaders will plan routes, hide sites, observation posts, and other tactical activities away from NLDs. Since NLDs are routes that locals frequently take, Marines normally make every effort to avoid them to avoid detection and limit the risk of being observed and compromised. In fact, for groups such as snipers, being too close to NLDs can prove fatal. When analyzing terrain with an offensive mindset, Marines use NLDs to establish ambush sites since the enemy may often follow NLDs when patrolling. Like Marines planning an ambush, combat profilers should consider NLDs as something to be exploited. NLDs indicate how people move through a neighborhood, tree line, or other types of terrain. Enemy personnel use NLDs just like the rest of the local populace. For combat profilers, NLDs show how people use the surrounding terrain. Furthermore, when observing NLDs, combat profilers can use the other domains (biometrics and kinesics) to identify potential anomalies. Proxemically, anyone who avoids NLDs should also be considered an anomaly.

The concept of NLDs is not just theoretical; it's a principle that criminals live by. A Los Angeles police department officer who has spent the majority of his career studying and combating gang violence in the Hollenbeck District tells about a time early in his career when he would chase gang members through alleyways. The gang members knew the locations of all the foot holes in walls and fences that could be used to help them jump these obstacles and keep one step ahead of the pursuing police. "Individuals, including criminals, do not move randomly through their environment."[144] Over time, this gang officer had studied his area so thoroughly that he knew all the side streets and alley getaways, knew where most of the gang members lived or would go to hide, and was able to operate as effectively in that area as the criminals themselves.

The principle of natural lines of drift can be applied in combat zones by looking at an area of operation to find creative ways to target insurgents. Homegrown insurgents will always know their neighborhoods and villages better than our deployed forces. An insurgent planting an IED will not transit by main roads or heavily patrolled byways. He'll use obscure alleys and back streets, and if he's spotted, he'll know all the "trap doors" and escape routes to make his getaway.

Finding these natural lines of drift is extremely important and can often be done by incorporating the art of tracking into your patrols as a way to determine how many people travel a certain path, how often they come through, and the last time that they were there. Once you have found these pathways around an area where you think an ambush may occur, you will be able to respond much more quickly in predicting how the enemy will leave the area, allowing you to cut off his escape routes.

Habitual Areas and Anchor Points

To the combat profiler, individuals congregate in one of two places: habitual areas and anchor points.

A habitual area is a place where anyone can come or go at any time. An anchor point is the opposite. An anchor point is a place whose ownership has been claimed by a particular person or group, either formally or informally, and is identified by the existence of pre-established criteria to gain entry. The local mall is a habitual area. Tony Soprano's Bada Bing Club is an anchor point.

Habitual Areas

The function of habitual areas is the same all over the world. Although a mall in America looks different than a bazaar in the Middle East, both places exist to provide the necessary commodities that people need to live. National attire may differ, and the types of products for sale may vary, but the layout and design of markets (or other similar places) is often very similar across cultures. Human behavior, regardless of location, will display a great number of parallels. The student combat profiler doesn't need to travel to Bangladesh or Burkina Faso to learn his trade. We can learn a lot right here at home. Developing thick file folders for American settings can go a long way toward increasing a combat profiler's recognition capabilities and decision-making abilities. Instead of focusing on differences between cultures, the student combat profiler should focus on the similarities in human behavior at these locations.

Because the insurgencies our country has been fighting for the last decade are people- and population-centric fights, Marines on patrol naturally operate in crowded and heavily populated areas. Because of that, Marines often find themselves in the marketplaces and gathering sites to interact with locals. The catch is that Marines aren't the only ones attracted to these areas. Criminals and insurgents also view habitual areas as places of opportunity. In such settings, bad guys will of course do their best to blend in with the locals. Once a Marine has established a baseline for the habitual area, he can then begin observing and hunting for the anomalies. The "wolves in sheep's clothing" will easily stand out because their behavior will not fit the baseline.

Habitual areas are points of attraction (markets, bazaars, public squares), but there will also be points within habitual areas that have restricted access and that people seek to avoid. In any city (habitual area), you will find neighborhoods where not everyone feels welcome. In outdoor markets that are open to the public, there will be stores and booths where only certain people are permitted. The next section will discuss the category we call Anchor Points, where not everyone is welcome. It is important for the combat profiler to understand that within neighborhoods, malls, city streets, buildings, and even a single room, there are always locations that are off-limits to outsiders.

Anchor Points

Consider a family's house. Under one roof are both habitual areas (kitchen, living room, bathroom) and anchor points. The parents may not allow everyone to enter their bedroom. Dad may have a study or workshop that others enter at their own risk. Teenagers, of course, are universally protective of their "private" space.

One level higher, the house itself may be considered the family's anchor point—the place from which the family as a whole operates, and within whose walls only certain outsiders are welcome. Moving up a few levels, a town or village possesses both habitual areas and anchor points. Habitual areas include the downtown area and the market. Anchor points are those areas to which only certain people are permitted access. A gang-controlled area of a neighborhood is a type of anchor point.

An anchor point is a home base. It's the place from which a person or group operates. An anchor point may be identified by the volume of traffic coming and going—and by the emotional attachment it evokes in those who "belong." It is the place that a person or group visits regularly, and it's often the most important place in that person's or group's life.

For most people, their home is their anchor point.[145] Criminals and insurgents may not necessarily use their home as an anchor point, but may have some other location from which they operate. These anchor points may be fixed or mobile, temporary, or permanent. Most crime happens in the vicinity of a criminal's anchor point, in those areas with which he or she is most familiar.[146] The same can be assumed for insurgents. Since insurgents often work in teams, they usually operate from some type of centralized base. That base is their anchor point.

Identifying anchor points will help the combat profiler to develop a baseline from which to predict human behavior. The question becomes, how are anchor points identified? Anchor points are not identified by their location and often not even by the way the place looks. Anchor points are identified based upon *the behavior of the people at that location*. The following are behavioral characteristics and patterns that can help to identify anchor points:

1. Only certain people have access to the location. Visitors are vetted. Strangers must meet some type of screening criteria to be granted permission to enter.

2. The place is protected and defended. Access is controlled by security personnel such as doormen or bouncers. Lookouts or outposts may provide early warning of any unauthorized approach. Should someone gain access who is not welcome, there will be retaliation for trespassing.

3. Locals in the area who know of the anchor point may go out of their way to avoid it. In this instance, we see simultaneously both the proxemic push of repulsion to outsiders and the proxemic pull of members being drawn to the location.

Human beings are territorial. Groups take possession of space. Nations have borders; gangs have turf. Whenever we observe "behavior characterized by identification with a geographic area in a way that indicates ownership," we also expect that ownership to involve "defense of that territory against perceived invaders."[147] People will fight for what is theirs.

Temporary Anchor Points

Anchor points don't always come in the form of buildings, and they don't have to be established for long periods of time. Two gang members take a position on a street corner, talking loudly and making a scene. How comfortable will people feel walking past with small children? That corner has become a temporary anchor point. When the gang members move away, the temporary anchor point vanishes with them, reverting to being a habitual area.

Temporary anchor points are quite common. You will see them whenever a person or group occupies an area for a limited time, such as park benches, a spot on the beach with chairs and towels, seats on public transportation, tables at an outdoor café, or a place in line.

Criminal vs. Personal Anchor Points

All criminals and insurgents have anchor points, but not all anchor points are criminal. The home of an underground leader, for instance, may be a personal anchor point, in that the leader will not be available to the population in that location. A religious leader may be willing to talk to anybody while he is at the religious center, but may still consider his private residence to be off limits. A person's home will become an anchor point for a variety of reasons, but isn't necessarily a criminal anchor point.

Combat profilers should focus their searches on criminal and insurgent anchor points. Criminals and insurgents need a haven where they feel secure in conducting their planning and preparations, whether it is a member's home, a local bar or meeting place, a safe house, etc. This location will also be the place to which the criminal returns immediately following the crime. To target criminals and insurgents effectively, the combat profiler must be able to identify these sanctuaries and force them to move by removing their perception of security. People are always more vulnerable on the move, and if we continue to eliminate safe havens and anchor points for criminals, our ability to neutralize and eliminate them will increase exponentially.

Finding Criminal Anchor Points

Criminals and insurgents are not going to make identifying their anchor points easy. Every care will be taken to conceal such "secure" areas. Combat profilers must search for cues that are often extremely subtle and covert.

Locals may unwittingly reveal the location of anchor points by walking out of their way to avoid a certain building or block within their village. In the language of combat profiling, this is a proxemic push.

Marines on patrol must remain alert to changes in the body language of locals as the patrol approaches a seemingly innocent location. Do people move away? Does their demeanor alter from comfortable and open to uncomfortable and defensive?

Graffiti, flags, or other insignia may indicate the presence of a criminal or insurgent anchor point.

Buffer space is another characteristic that can help us locate an anchor point. A buffer zone is the "demilitarized" area surrounding an anchor point. This space provides the criminal or insurgent with a level of comfort and security. Criminals and insurgents do not usually conduct crimes and attacks within this space because of the risk of getting caught or of having their anchor point identified. Butch Cassidy did not rob trains within a hundred miles of his hideout at Hole in the Wall. The criminal is protecting his neighbors as well, by not bringing hostile security forces into their backyard, as he expects these neighbors to shield him by keeping their mouths shut. The buffer zone keeps criminals and insurgents from "operating too close to home."[148]

The combat profiler should look for areas that, though surrounded by instances of criminal activity, remain remarkably immune to attacks and crime. This may be an indicator of an anchor point surrounded by a buffer zone. Visual assessment of this area may then confirm the presence of an anchor point based on the behavior of locals and the people at the assumed anchor point.

The reward for identifying criminal and insurgent anchor points will be an exponential increase in the effectiveness of patrols and other security operations. By forcing the insurgents to react to our presence and actions and removing the security they were seeking when they established their anchor point will allow us to maintain offensive and proactive actions in the hunt.

Geographics in History

Before his death in 2011, there had been two very public attempts on Osama bin Laden's life since September 11, 2001. The first one was executed in December 2001 in Tora Bora, a mountainous region on Afghanistan's eastern border, dubbed Operation Anaconda. The assault began with Afghan troops supported by U.S. Special Operations forces and American aerial bombing, followed a few days later by an area sweep conducted by soldiers of the U.S. 10th Mountain Division. Ultimately, bin Laden escaped this hunt, but the concept of geographics can provide us with an instructive picture of the episode.

Tora Bora was an anchor point. It was a place where Osama bin Laden felt secure. Tora Bora was surrounded by a buffer zone. Bin Laden could eat, sleep, confer with confederates, and plan operations, knowing that he had abundant early warning of transgressors. Tora Bora was close to the Pakistan border, should the Al-Qaeda leader need to flee the country, and the area was filled with loyal followers willing to defend him against any attackers. Operation Anaconda failed by not securing a cordon around the village and blocking the egress routes leading out of Tora Bora. In the mission plan, this task was left mostly to the Afghan forces, and while they did establish checkpoints on the main routes, due to a lack of sufficient manpower, they left mountain trails and "goat paths" unsecured.

During the course of the fight, Osama bin Laden was escorted out of Tora Bora by forty to fifty fighters who had an extensive knowledge of the area and who used the natural lines of drift (those goat paths) to get him out fast. According to reports after the operation in Tora Bora, many believe that bin Laden did not return to Pakistan as originally thought. With an American bounty on his head, he did not feel safe in that country. Instead, it is believed that he went north towards Jalalabad and established a new anchor point. The key criterion in creating an anchor point is the ability to ensure security and exclusivity of access. As history shows, bin Laden correctly assessed that the tribes in Jalalabad would provide better security than what he would have received in Pakistan, as he remained free for almost another decade.[149]

Consider how the concepts of combat profiling helped ultimately to locate and kill Osama bin Laden. The primary search was for bin Laden's anchor point. This ended with the identification of a compound in Abbottabad, Pakistan. Instead of the mountain cave that many in U.S. intelligence predicted would be his hideout, bin Laden was holed up on the third floor of a million-dollar compound that had twelve foot-high concrete walls topped with barbed wire, further protected by two security fences. Besides the obvious protection, the anomalies began to mount. U.S. agencies discovered that the compound lacked a phone or Internet connection, though such amenities could be acquired with ease in affluent Abbottabad. Observers discovered that the walled compound burned its own trash instead of putting it out for collection like the rest of the town. This, along with other evidence, allowed our intelligence agencies to focus their search on that building to confirm their assumptions. As they were planning the raid, they kept in mind the natural lines of drift that Bin Laden could use to escape and kept a helicopter-borne response force on stand-by should they need reinforcements for an immediate search if bin Laden managed to escape the house.[150]

Abbottabad itself was a habitual area that Pakistanis would go to visit during the heat of the summer, but it was the act of sorting through the people there and identifying it as an anchor point with key anomalies that allowed the Americans to target the most wanted terrorist in the world. The successful result of the attack shows how geographics can help us narrow our focus from a large habitual area, in this case, an entire region of the globe, into smaller observable segments and make more educated plans and decisions.

Geographics Summary

If the combat profiler can identify an anchor point, habitual areas, and NLDs, he or she can begin to predict human behavior within a geographic area. A baseline can be established even before he or she enters the location. This will greatly reduce the time it takes to orient himself or herself to any potential threats or anomalies. This will increase our predictive and therefore proactive nature on the battlefield.

Understanding these geographical concepts allows us to further understand and forecast criminal acts. We know that bad guys will leave their anchor point, whether it is their home or a safe house, when they are ready to conduct their next crime. The crime will likely occur in a habitual area, whose terrain they are familiar with and within whose population they both feel secure and can blend in. They will use NLDs both to approach their target and to withdraw from it.

Additionally, we know that bad guys don't just target habitual areas, but they choose also to target areas that they are familiar with, which offer them an increased level of confidence in the ultimate success of their crime. Understanding the relationship that people have with their environment can let you predict human behavior and movement long before an action takes place. It is a crucial aspect of understanding humans.

Geographics Takeaways

1. People act differently in an area depending on whether they are familiar or unfamiliar with the environment.

2. NLDs are the pathways that people take that allow for a simple and safe movement from point A to point B while exerting the least amount of effort.

3. Habitual areas are places where any person can visit without restriction.

4. Anchor points are places where only people who meet an exclusive set of requirements are granted access.

5. Anchor points can be identified by places where access is controlled.

6. Identifying criminal anchor points is the focus of effort for security forces seeking to disrupt criminal, insurgent, and terrorist activities.

7. ICONOGRAPHY

Iconography is visual language.

We see it everywhere: as symbols on T-shirts, tattoos, graffiti on buildings, traffic signs, advertisements, and the images companies use to identify and market their products.

An icon is any symbol used to promote a person's or group's presence, beliefs, or affiliations. Individuals and groups use iconography to draw allies and converts to them, to intimidate enemies and drive them away, to further their agendas, to boast, to brag, to bully, and to buffalo. Iconography often communicates complex messages through simple pictures, symbols, and writing. But why should combat profilers pay heed to iconography?

Iconography is not directly an aspect of human behavior. It is not driven by the limbic system or autonomic processes. Iconography, particularly personal iconography, is easily masked or hidden (e.g., tattoos) or changed (e.g., clothing). We include iconography as one of the domains because combat profilers can use iconography to increase their situational awareness.

Paying attention to iconography opens the combat profiler's eyes to messages being communicated by symbols in the environment. By analyzing and understanding the iconography present in any human situation, the combat profiler can determine the beliefs of an individual or group. He can tell that person or group's affiliation. Who are their allies? Who are their enemies? What do they stand for? Combat profilers can observe iconography to understand what things are important in an area to individuals and groups and what elements are influencing the people in an area. By identifying the changes in iconography over time, combat profilers can understand how and in which direction a political, social, or military situation is trending.

Iconography can be divided into two realms: indicators that appear on people and indicators that appear in geographical environments.

In a geographical environment, iconography can tell us:

1. The intent or beliefs of those who imprinted the iconography,
2. Whether groups in the area are in conflict, and
3. The relationship between the people who live in the area and the people who left the iconography.

Regarding this last point, there is a significant difference between allowing the iconography to remain in place (e.g., graffiti or political or religious slogans scrawled on walls) and taking action to eradicate it or paint over it. In the first case, the community tolerates and may actively embrace the beliefs and agenda of those imprinting the iconography. In the second, the local population resists or is attempting to disassociate itself from the purveyors of the iconography.

The iconography that individuals display on their person also provides important information. First, we can determine what types of things a person supports or doesn't support, particularly if the iconography displays a negative message about something. Second, we can tell what a person's associations are. Third, we can tell a person's status or assumed status (i.e., what they believe their status is).

Personal iconography is important to the average person, but significantly more important to the criminal: "It bears emphasizing that especially in the criminal population, symbols and external markings acquire tenfold meaning and have great value and a significant function."[151] The criminal world often uses symbols that are considered illicit or illegitimate in the law-abiding world. Criminals choose symbols that often go against the norm.[152]

There are three main categories of iconography that combat profilers should be aware of: graffiti and other forms of public iconography, tattoos, and clothing and other artifacts.

Graffiti

Graffiti is any writing or drawing on a public place done without the consent of the owner of the space.

Three types of graffiti are of concern to the combat profiler: territorial graffiti (tagging done by groups to identify their territory), political and ideological graffiti

(graffiti which expresses some type of political or belief statement), and threatening graffiti (graffiti that menaces or attempts to intimidate others, specifically local or foreign security forces, or inspires others to do so).

Territorial graffiti is used by gangs and similar groups to let outsiders know that they are trespassing on turf claimed by the gang. Often a gang's territory is marked by boundary graffiti, which indicates the limits of the gang's home ground. Graffiti increases the more deeply one penetrates to the heart of the territory.[153] Graffiti is often a real-time indicator of local attitudes, and as one study argues, graffiti can be a "prelude and a directive to open behavior and clues to the bounds and intensity of a community's control of its territory."[154]

Other public iconography includes artifacts such as flags, signs, even colors. These are often indicators of what type of groups are operating in an area, or what type of groups the people in the area support. Flags are prominent means of providing group identity and solidarity. A flag advertises a group's presence in an area; it establishes a rallying point for the group's members. Flags are also often rich in symbolism. Many provide extensive clues to the values and ideologies of the group.

Consider the symbols and colors of the American flag. The various Taliban flags, which have been used since that group emerged in the early 1990s, have not only served as icons but also have by their presence made powerful political statements. After a battle between U.S. and Taliban forces in late 2009, the Taliban raised a flag in the province of Nuristan in eastern Afghanistan as a statement of what they claimed was a victory.[155] This was a significant attempt by the Taliban to influence the local people—an act demonstrating their power and their claim to ownership of the area. In contrast, forces loyal to the Afghan government raised their national flag over the city of Marjah to demonstrate their victory over Taliban forces in early 2010.[156]

In addition to flags, other public iconography includes the simple display of colors. The blue bandana of the Crips and the red of the Bloods are recognized in every American city. In recent years, businesses in Los Angeles with ties to terrorist groups in the Arab world have begun displaying colors with Middle Eastern significance. Colors are often given meaning by the groups that use them. Red frequently carries the meaning of sacrifice, due to its association with blood. White often indicates purity. Black may indicate death. The key is to understand the significance of colors in whatever area you are operating. In addition to flags and colors, any sign, flyer, or other public symbol should be assessed to determine its significance.

Tattoos

Because tattoos are permanent, they often possess extremely significant meaning for the wearer. The location on the person's body may be meaningful as well.[157] Tattoos are meant to gain attention and to communicate a message.[158] The most important for the combat profiler include:

1. Membership in a group, specifically a gang, insurgent/terrorist operation, or extremist organization.
2. Association or identification with a specific cause, especially one that espouses violence.
3. Symbols representing past incarceration.

The number of Americans with tattoos remains relatively small—perhaps at most, six to fifteen percent of all

Americans.[159] However, the number of tattooed individuals who are or have been in prison is significantly higher—thirty-two percent.[160]

A study, which focused on the relationship between tattoos and the criminal way of life, found that criminals get tattoos for reasons such as "self-indulgence, a need for gratification, a deep commitment to delinquency and criminality and a disregard of their consequences" and concluded that tattoos endorse the criminal lifestyle.[161]

Tattoos have been shown to be associated with high-risk behavior.[162] Several studies have linked tattoos with "deviance, personality disorders, substance abuse, risk-taking behavior, and criminality."[163] One scholar writes, "The criminal world universally considers tattoos an inseparable part of their symbols."[164]

If a person has a visible tattoo, it does not mean that he or she is or will be a criminal or a threat; however, a tattoo is certainly one indicator, which may mark an individual as an anomaly worthy of further observation. For example, in Iraq, certain groups of insurgent fighters wore tattoos of three small dots forming a triangle on one of their hands. Observing this would immediately warrant further observation or questioning of the individual.

Clothing and Other Artifacts

Humans across all cultures use clothing and other artifacts (e.g., jewelry, badges, accessories, emblems, and images on clothing) to communicate associations, beliefs, and status. Gangs, teams, military forces, insurgent organizations, and other organized groups often wear some type of clothing or emblem unique to them. This is "branding." It is done to allow group members to identify one another, to provide a sense of unity and solidarity, as well as to distinguish the group from other competing groups.

Often the emblems chosen have symbolic significance—they tell a story of the group's beliefs, origins, goals, or other important aspects of collective ideology.

Individuals select clothing and other artifacts to communicate messages to others. On the day that Timothy McVeigh was arrested—the same day he blew up the Murrah Federal Building in Oklahoma City—he was wearing a T-shirt with a picture of Abraham Lincoln on the front and the Latin phrase *Sic Semper Tyrannis* ("Thus always to tyrants"). On the back was a quote attributed to Thomas Jefferson: "The tree of liberty must be refreshed from time to time with the blood of patriots and tyrants." John Wilkes Booth was said to have cried, *"Sic semper tyrannis"* after shooting Abraham Lincoln. McVeigh wore the shirt because it displayed his ideology, which drove his decision to attack a federal building and kill almost 170 people.

Individuals within groups also distinguish themselves by their clothing and other emblems. Videos of insurgent leaders often show the insurgent leader with clothing, jewelry, weaponry, or other items that set them apart from their subordinates. Gangs in the U.S. wear clothes, which in some form or fashion, exhibit symbols that represent their gang—these symbols may be specific colors or certain professional sports emblems.

A recent study reported that drivers who displayed bumper stickers ("territorial markers") were significantly more likely to exhibit road rage and other aggressive behavior. "It appears that the mere presence of territory markers has predictive value in determining aggressive driving, as does the number of territory markers."[165] Although the study was not able to confirm that hostile bumper stickers were related to more aggressive driving, it is not too far of a stretch to suspect that individuals who display hostile or threatening messages may be more prone to aggressive action than others who display neutral or friendly messages. A bumper sticker that reads "Violence solves everything" is a much different message than one that reads "Embrace peace."

Iconographic Baselines and Anomalies

Iconography is not a behavioral indicator like biometrics, kinesics, or proxemics. Rather, iconography is a deliberate display, communicated via signs and symbols, of a person or group's associations and beliefs. Combat profilers should immediately begin to assess the iconographic baseline for any location in which they operate. Combat profilers should look for patterns in the iconography of the environment: What groups are represented? Are the messages positive or negative? How do the locals respond to the iconography?

A population will either support, tolerate, or reject messages communicated through public iconography. If the locals support the group and its messages, they will demonstrate this through their behavior. They will begin to mimic the messages, signs, and symbols. They may display the iconography themselves. They will be proxemically drawn to it. Locals who simply tolerate the iconography will not mimic the messages but will continue to allow the iconography to be displayed. Locals who reject the iconography will attempt to conceal or destroy it, e.g., painting over graffiti. Additionally, if the iconography is offensive, or if the locals are intimidated by the group that has created and displayed it, locals may be proxemically pushed away from the iconography and may exhibit signs of discomfort around it.

There are two main anomalies related to iconography. The first anomaly is the sudden appearance of or change in iconography. New types of graffiti may pop up in an area or the messages of the graffiti may change. For example, local iconography display messages that are supportive of the local security force but then suddenly begin communicating negative messages. The second type of anomaly is the attempt to hide or conceal the iconography when Marines or security forces are present. Both of these anomalies relate to public iconography (graffiti, flags, etc.) and personal iconography (tattoos, logos on clothing, etc.). Both of these types of anomalies should be warning flags to combat profilers.

Combat profilers should be aware that clothing and other artifacts can often distinguish leaders within groups, and that people communicate messages about themselves based on their clothing and artifacts. We should not ignore the messages that individuals broadcast to those around them. Symbols have meaning. Because certain iconography can be concealed or removed, it may not be identifiable or present in all circumstances; however, being aware of the messages displayed through iconography can make a combat profiler significantly more aware of his or her surroundings.

ICONOGRAPHY Takeaways

1. Iconography is not an uncontrollable element of human behavior, so it can be easily masked or concealed, and sometimes requires significant interpretation.
2. Iconography can be geographic or personal and conveys a person or group's beliefs and affiliations.
3. Graffiti, flags, signs, banners, and posters are often used to mark territory (affiliation) but also convey the beliefs of the group that posted the message.
4. Tattoos and clothing are used for the same purpose but are personal displays of their beliefs or associations.

8. ATMOSPHERICS

The last domain of combat profiling is atmospherics. Atmospherics can be defined as the collective mood of a situation or place. On June 2, 1967, Company D, 1st Battalion, 5th Marines and Company F, 2nd Battalion, 5th Marines were patrolling toward an objective near the village of Vihn Huy in Vietnam. As both companies advanced across a rice paddy, the villagers, normally active, seemed silent and still. Livestock and domestic animals did not move. Even the birds went silent. Suddenly, the NVA launched an ambush. Patrick Haley, an anti-tank assaultman with Company F, described the moment before the attack as "too quiet, too serene...you could almost smell the presence of the enemy."[166]

The collective mood is the combination of the individual moods and emotions of people in an environment. This mood is displayed primarily through nonverbal behavior (biometric, kinesic, and proxemic cues), geographic indicators, iconography, and other indicators.

Atmospherics is not some mystical feeling or indefinable vibe. Though we may first experience the atmosphere of a situation through an instinct or a feeling, by employing the science of atmospherics, we can break that gut sense down into definable, observable indicators.

Combat profiling is about having situational awareness and proactively identifying threats. Being able to read the mood of a situation is part of having situational awareness. The inability to pick up on the atmospherics of a situation can be deadly, like the customer who strolls into a convenience store and shops without any clue that a robbery is in progress or the cop who walks into a gas station and does not pick up on the fact that the cashier is being robbed at gunpoint. A Marine patrol may fail to pick up on the hostile mood of a village—displayed by the locals through negative body language and proxemic pushes—which could indicate an imminent attack.

Emotions are Honest

Atmospherics is not hocus-pocus. The concept of collective mood is a concrete reality. The combination of individual moods and emotions in a situation creates this collective mood.[167] Moods and emotions are true responses to a situation or event. When people seem anxious, tense, or afraid, it is likely that something has occurred or is present that is making them feel and act that way.

Emotions and moods are driven by autonomic and subconscious processes in the brain.[168] The part of the brain responsible for picking up on other people's emotions is the amygdala. The amygdala is part of the limbic system. It is also responsible for detecting potential threats and for preparing the body's necessary physiological responses and actions.[169] Because moods and emotions are first experienced subconsciously, in any given situation, we will initially "feel" what is going on before we become consciously aware of it. Being attuned to your own emotional response in any situation can increase the speed at which you cognitively understand what is going on. This is why we often say things such as, "The situation felt tense," or "Patrolling through that village made me feel uneasy." We feel the emotion and mood that is expressed through the behavior of others. That behavior is a true indicator of the emotions people are feeling, which is an honest response to something that has either happened, is present, or is about to happen.

Moods are Contagious

Moods and emotions are also contagious. They pass from one person to another subconsciously through mimicry and other means. This is true particularly of negative emotions. One person with a negative emotion (anger, anxiety, fear, etc.) can infect a large group.[170] People mimic others around them; when one person copies another's behavior, the second person will begin to experience the first person's emotion.[171] When an individual senses something and has an emotional reaction such as fear, anxiety, or anger, that person's emotional state can affect everyone else.[172]

There are two categories of atmospherics: positive and negative. Just because a place or situation exhibits a positive atmosphere does not mean that we can let our guard down. We must always be suspicious. To borrow Gavin de Becker's idea, we must always have the mindset that "An attack will always occur right now."[173] So even when the atmosphere is positive, combat profilers must constantly look for anomalies and threats.

A negative atmosphere, conversely, should serve as an immediate alarm that something is wrong. Negative moods and emotions can be categorized as sadness, anxiety, fear, anger, hostility, and contempt.

Atmospheric Baselines and Anomalies

As in the other domains, the combat profiler uses atmospheric indicators to establish a baseline. Every place or situation possesses an emotional atmosphere. This atmosphere will be a true indicator of the emotions and attitudes of the people in the situation.

Once the emotional atmosphere of a situation is determined, combat profilers should begin to consciously identify the behavioral indicators that are creating the atmosphere. Even when we are not physically part of an event—say, when we are observing from a distance—we can still determine the atmospheric baseline by reading the indicators discussed below.

When we are a part of a situation, we will reason first from "feel," then confirm our assessment based on observable indicators. When we are observing from a distance, we don't have the luxury of "feel." We must determine the atmosphere of a situation based entirely on indicators.

Biometrics and Kinesics

Since mood and emotion are primarily communicated through nonverbal behavior, these two domains will most likely provide the main indicators. Displays of positive nonverbal behavior communicate a positive atmosphere. A negative atmosphere will be characterized by negative body language—arms crossed, aggressive stances, clenched fists, facial expressions of anger or contempt, people leaning away if sitting down, etc.

Proxemics

Interpersonal distance can be a key clue to the atmosphere in a situation. People avoiding or keeping their distance from something or someone may indicate fear or anxiety about whatever they are avoiding. The key is to identify what it is that people are avoiding or keeping their distance from. Aggressive movements toward something or quick movements away from something may also indicate danger or a potential threat.

Iconography

The messages displayed in an environment set a mood or tone for that area. The iconography displayed in an area tells us about the beliefs and affiliations of whoever painted, posted, broadcast, or wore the iconography. Additionally, the messages and mood communicated by the iconography have an effect upon those who are exposed to it.

Noise Level

Every place or situation has certain noises and sounds associated with it. When you walk into your home, you expect to hear certain sounds. When those sounds are altered or absent, you know something is different, perhaps dangerous. The same goes for a street in Los Angeles, a bazaar in Afghanistan, or a key leader engagement in the Middle East.

Silence may be explained by two phenomena: lack of noise or auditory exclusion. Auditory exclusion occurs when your brain begins to shut down or reduce your ability to hear any sound or certain sounds in stressful situations. This is related to the tunnel vision discussed in the biometrics section. Your body diverts energy and attention toward the threat or potential threat and reduces or cuts off unneeded avenues of information. This is why many individuals report hearing nothing, or hearing muffled sounds, during situations such as a firefight. Studies have shown that between fifty-one and eighty-four percent of law enforcement officers involved in shootings remember experiencing diminished sound perception.[174] True silence can occur because people in an area have fled or hidden themselves because of fear or because tension or dread has caused people to become silent. Either way, lack of noise in an area or situation in which noise should be present should be taken as an immediate warning.

Activity

Downtown Kabul is busy during the daytime. The Wall Street Stock Exchange is a madhouse. But people don't generally move frantically and display agitated behavior in places such as a mosque or a funeral home. The category of activity can also include activity over time such as shops opening and closing at a certain time or times of busy traffic. It is critical to identify the baseline patterns of activity in a location so that you can identify changes. The behavior and level of activity in an area should fit the situation and environment; any deviation from the norm is an anomaly.

Order and Disorder

The concept of order and disorder can be applied to a physical environment or to a crowd or group.

In a physical environment, order and disorder refer to the way the area looks and whether or not rules are being followed in the area. A recent study has provided support for the "Broken Window Theory." This report confirmed that even one element of disorder in an area (e.g., graffiti, the sound of fireworks in an area in which fireworks are banned, or even something as simple as bicycles chained to a fence) creates further disorder—even criminal activity.[175]

Regarding a group, order and disorder refer to the group's behavior. An orderly march or demonstration is obviously different from a hostile and chaotic riot. Between these two extremes exist various levels of order and disorder. The more disorderly a group's behavior, the greater the possibility for violence.

Determining Anomalies

There are three main types of anomalies associated with atmospherics:

1. An immediate negative atmosphere. Often the combat profiler may not have the time or ability to determine the atmospheric baseline of an area. Many times, we simply have to respond based on the current atmosphere without extensive observation.

Because this is the case, we should take any negative atmosphere as an indicator that something may be wrong.

2. The individual who does not fit the atmosphere. Because mood is contagious and emotions are honest, we should expect that people's moods and emotions will match each other and fit that situation. We should consider any person an anomaly when their attitude, emotion or mood, and/or behavior does not fit what is expected for a situation.

3. A sudden change in mood. In combat profiling, this is called an *atmospheric shift*. Atmospheric shifts can be both positive and negative. We are primarily concerned with negative atmospheric shifts, but any sudden shift in the atmosphere of a situation should make us take a closer look for other indicators, as well as for whatever caused the atmospheric shift.

Atmospheric Shifts

Like ripples in a pond caused by the splashing of a stone, atmospheric shifts are the emotional and situational reactions to a development in a situation, such as a person entering an area, something said, or something done. We see things like this on a daily basis. A group of Marines casually talking or interacting will immediately change their behavior as soon as an officer or senior enlisted Marine approaches. Office employees exhibit the same behavior while chatting around the water cooler when the boss approaches. Talking turns to silence, and slouching turns to sitting or standing upright. This same type of behavior was observed by a research team in Afghanistan conducting interviews. At one point during an interview with a young Afghan woman, "She suddenly stopped talking and covered her face with her *chador* when her soon-to-be mother-in-law stepped into the room. She turned her covered face away from the mother-in-law, and did not say another word."[176] When observing an atmospheric shift, it is important to identify whether the shift was positive or negative, but it is more important to identify *what caused* the atmospheric shift. The change in atmosphere is the indicator; what changed the atmosphere is most likely the threat.

There are two types of atmospheric shifts: positive and negative. That is, the atmosphere of an environment can go from a negative to a positive mood (a positive atmospheric shift) or from a positive to a negative mood (a negative atmospheric shift). Combat profilers should be concerned primarily with negative atmospheric shifts, since they are more likely indicators of a potential threat. For instance, Marines on patrol may be effectively speaking with locals until a Taliban member (unknown to the Marines) approaches. At this point, locals may shut down and stop conversing because they feel intimidated by the individual approaching. Negative atmospheric shifts may be caused by an increase in tension, anxiety, fear, or anger. Indicators of a negative atmospheric shift may be displays of defensive or aggressive body language, increased proxemic distance, or silence or stopped conversation.

Combat profilers must recognize that they themselves may be the cause of an atmospheric shift. When this happens, a new atmospheric baseline will be established until the combat profiler leaves the area or situation. Further atmospheric shifts may also occur due to the combat profiler's actions or the presence or entry of another individual.

By identifying atmospherics, combat profilers can gain an immediate understanding for the moods, emotions, and attitudes of people in any given situation. By quickly establishing a baseline, using one's intuition and identifying observable indicators, combat profilers can more quickly pick up on anomalies. Combat profilers should be concerned primarily with negative atmospheric moods and negative atmospheric shifts because these are related to potential threats.

Atmospherics Takeaways*

1. Atmospherics is the collective mood of a situation or place and can provide an immediate indication of safety or danger.

2. Atmospherics are made up of information gained from the other domains, the noise level, the level of activity, and the sense of order or disorder in the area.

3. Positive atmospherics indicate a sense of security.

4. Negative atmospherics are often a "left of bang" indicator of a threat.

5. Negative atmospheric shifts are sudden changes in an area from a "positive" feel to a "negative" feel. They should alert the combat profiler to a significant change in the area.

---

*To view and download the indicators that make up each of these domains, visit: www.cp-journal.com/leftofbang

PART FOUR

TAKING ACTION

1. DECIDING TO ACT

Making decisions in combat has never been easy. It's a heck of a lot easier when the enemy is wearing a distinguishable uniform and is directly in front of you. There is no doubt that the Marines and soldiers during World War II or the Korean War had it rough. Modern Marines rarely find themselves rushing a machine-gun bunker or wading through eight hundred meters of surf in an attempt to attack a heavily fortified small island. At least in conventional warfare, the enemy is obvious, whereas in today's irregular warfare, the enemy can be anywhere at anytime and is often not distinguishable from the surrounding populace. It's safe to say that making decisions is much more difficult in the complex, chaotic whirlwind of an environment in which the modern Marine, or soldier, finds himself today.

In today's combat environment, often the only visible clues of enemy presence or activity are subtle indicators—children not playing outside, locals avoiding a certain stretch of road, or villagers acting less friendly than usual. The enemy, by and large, doesn't wear a uniform, doesn't declare his intentions, and doesn't stand out from the crowd. Instead, he attempts to blend with the rest of the population. The enemy does his best to mask his intentions, conceal his actions, and make every effort to attack Marines and soldiers at the time and location of his (the enemy's) choosing. Marines returning from combat have described this reality repeatedly. One combat vet described the challenge on the ground with:

*What makes this job difficult is that you can't easily distinguish a group of
ordinary people doing their ordinary business from armed groups. In an
insurgency, you are dealing with civilian-clothed opponents. It's hard to tell who
are the Taliban. I am sure there are hard-core elements, but because of the nature
of the society, one day you are aligned to the Taliban, the next day, to somebody
else. The trick for them is to blend in with the locals. The Taliban use
communities to play hide and seek with us. Until they fire upon
our troops it's impossible to determine their motives. According to
the rules of engagement, that's the only time when it becomes
obvious who the enemy is.[177]*

As we discussed early on, combat profiling provides people with a way to make quick and accurate decisions. The combat profiling heuristic assists in making snap decisions with little time and with little information. The process for making decisions is simple: Establish the baseline, identify anomalies, decide, and act. The key to any decision-making is when to decide—the combat profiling heuristic says that three anomalies are enough to decide.

2. THE COMBAT RULE OF THREE

Any effective method of decision-making should have a threshold of decision. This is the point at which, no matter what, you *must* make a decision. A threshold of decision guards against hesitation and indecision due to overanalysis or waiting for additional information. The combat profiling threshold is called the *Combat Rule of Three*: When you observe three anomalies or indicators, you *must* make a decision. Do not wait for more information.

Three indicators are enough information with which to act. Does this mean that you must have three anomalies to make a decision? No. In some situations, one anomaly or indicator is sufficient. For instance, following the usual rules of engagement, if an individual exhibits a hostile act or hostile intent, one indicator is enough. Someone presenting a weapon in a hostile way toward a Marine on patrol or cop on the street is all it takes to engage that individual with deadly force.

Vehicle checkpoints often have a *trigger line*—a point at which if a vehicle crosses without first coming to a stop and being waved through by friendly force personnel, then the vehicle will automatically either be shot at (with a warning shot) or fully engaged by fire (again, this depends on the current escalation of force measures). But the trigger line serves as a threshold of decision—no more information is needed. Crossing the trigger line demonstrates a hostile act, and that is enough to make a decision. The reality is that no other information has to be collected in those situations. A Marine providing security for a checkpoint usually only has this one piece of information with which to work. Vehicles approaching a checkpoint with the intent to do harm to the security personnel at the checkpoint often travel at high rates of speed. There is no time to collect any other information. Marines can't converse with the driver or read his intent based on facial expressions or emotions. Yet, a decision must be made.

In the majority of situations, one indicator may not be enough. For instance, any Internet search of "deception detection" or "lie detection" will result in a host of pseudoscience websites and blogs that claim to tell you about how to detect if someone is lying. Many of them list certain "foolproof" indicators. Common among these foolproof indicators are fidgeting or shaking hands. These websites claim that you can tell that someone is lying based on one indicator—this just isn't true. Paul Ekman, the world's foremost expert on deception detection, writes in his book

Telling Lies, "People would lie less if they thought there was any such certain sign of lying, but there isn't. *There is no sign of deceit itself*—no gesture, facial expression, or muscle twitch that in and of itself means that a person is lying."[178]

In combat profiling, we look for a cluster of cues. We advocate making decisions based on three cues. Once three cues are identified, a decision must be made. The strength of a heuristic is that these decisions are pre-determined, and combat profiling provides three main decisions.

3. THE THREE DECISIONS

Before we discuss the three decisions, we should make it clear that the original purpose of combat profiling is to train *Marines* to be better and faster decision makers in combat. Therefore, the three decisions reflect that reality. Any application of combat profiling in other situations, by other security personnel, or even the average person wanting to be more aware and stay safe on a daily basis will have to adapt the decisions to their particular circumstances. On that note, the three decisions that a combat profiler may make are *Kill*, *Capture*, or *Contact*—in that order.

What does this mean? It doesn't mean that the first thing that combat profilers do is kill. It means that, in any given situation, in a potentially hostile environment, the first decision that combat profilers should make is to kill or *prepare* to kill. If an individual does not commit a hostile act, demonstrate hostile intent, or provide indicators of an immediate threat, then the combat profiler moves to the next decision—capture. If the individual does not give off indicators of a potential threat or if the person does not appear to be of significant intelligence value, then the combat profiler moves to the next and final decision—contact. If, for some reason, the individual gives off further indicators, then the combat profiler may move back up the decision tree to capture or kill if necessary. This simple decision tree can be depicted as such:

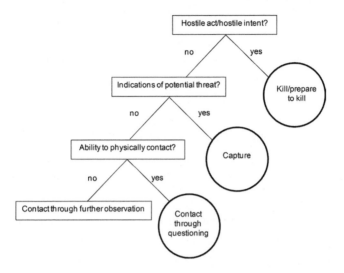

Before we briefly explain each of these decisions, we should discuss why our decision tree proceeds from the most violent decision to the least violent.

There are two main reasons why our decision making tree begins with the most violent course of action. First, humans have an internal reluctance to kill. In *On Killing*, Dave Grossman writes about the nature and effects of killing in humans, and states: "I began to realize that there was one major factor that was missing from the common understanding of killing in combat, a factor that answers this question and more. That missing factor is the simple and demonstrable fact that there is within most men an intense resistance to killing their fellow man. A resistance so strong that, in many circumstances, soldiers on the battlefield will die before they can overcome it."[179] It is difficult to say exactly why people are reluctant to kill, but as Grossman articulates, "There can be no doubt that this resistance to killing one's fellow man is there and that it exists as a result of a powerful combination of instinctive, rational, environmental, hereditary, cultural, and social factors."[180] This is certainly not to say that soldiers won't or don't kill, but that there is a strong reluctance to killing. Therefore, it is necessary in a combat environment, or other potentially hostile situation which may require responses of deadly force, to begin the decision tree with kill (or prepare to kill) to reduce any chance of rationalizing or backing down from making the tough choice of pulling the trigger.

The second, and more important, reason the decision tree begins with the most violent option is that, in combat environments, to not be prepared to take the most violent course of action is to put oneself at risk. In hostile situations, it is much easier to back down from a decision to kill than it is to ramp up to a decision to kill. Furthermore, if the situation is serious enough, and if the threat is immediate, then to cycle from contact to capture to kill wastes valuable time. One of the main purposes of combat profiling is to proactively identify threats—this especially means proactively identifying hostile people and preparing to take action once hostile indicators are present. Therefore, combat profilers should begin by assessing whether the most serious decision—kill—is required first, and then moving to the next, less serious, decision—capture.

The first decision—kill—certainly involves the act of killing (pulling the trigger) but also involves the mental determination and physical preparations to kill. Based on the observed indicators, the combat profiler may not have the opportunity to actually see any specific hostile act or hostile intent or be in the best position necessary to actually pull the trigger and kill the threat. When this is the case, the combat profiler must have the mindset that, when the conditions are right, or when the hostile act is exhibited or hostile intent is expressed, then he will immediately pull the trigger. Therefore, he must prepare to kill—mentally and physically.

The second decision—capture—means either physically subduing the targeted individual(s) or ensuring that the target cannot egress from the area and escape. This may necessitate physically cordoning off the area and having other individuals control exit points. At this point, the target has given off indicators of such a nature that detention and further questioning is necessary.

The third decision—contact—involves either physically contacting the individual through purposeful or casual questioning or continuing focused observation. At this point, the target has not given off sufficient indicators to be considered an immediate threat or in warrant physical detention, but they have presented themselves to be an anomaly and further investigation or observation is required. The purpose of contacting is to determine whether or not the individual is a potential threat or if the individual's anomalous behavior warrants any further action. If through either further observation or questioning the individual is determined to be benign, then the combat profiler lets the individual go and begins again to scan the environment for anomalies.

Decisions are situational. There are no decisions that will absolutely apply to all situations. As we stated above, the decisions kill, capture, contact are *only* intended to be applied by Marines in a combat situation. The decisions are *not* to be used outside of a combat situation. We cannot cover every type of situation in which a person may need to make a quick decision. Law enforcement personnel must select and employ a set of decisions that align with current law and their own official procedures. For civilians in noncombat situations we recommend "*run, hide, fight.*" For a civilian who encounters an attacker, the best chance for that person's survival is to put as much distance as possible between him or herself and the threat. The greater the separation the harder it is for an attacker to be effective, requiring a higher degree of skill to use a weapon effectively and to its fullest capability. When fleeing is not viable, the second option is to hide from the attacker and create as many barriers as possible to avoid being seen (concealment) and to find protection (cover). Finally, the third option exists for the times when all other chances of avoiding confrontation are no longer available. In this case, fighting the attacker through any means available may be the only chance of survival. This option is the last choice because it is inherently the most dangerous.

Some situations may require a different set of decisions, such as when an active shooter has entered into a school. Run, hide, fight is most effective when talking with adults who are able to fully understand and assess the situation, which isn't necessarily the case with small children. For teachers who find themselves in a situation with a shooter, the best course of action is to hide the students and attempt to keep the attacker out of the classroom. The reason we don't recommend that teachers try to evacuate the building with their students is because the risk of a child freezing in a hallway or in the face of an attacker is too high and could risk the lives of a greater number of students. That being said, we understand that every situation is unique and our goal with this book is to provide you with the greatest amount of time *left of bang* to recognize the situation and take the action that is best suited for the circumstances you are in.

PART FIVE

APPLICATIONS

1. BRINGING IT ALL TOGETHER

On Friday, January 3rd, 2014, 22-year-old Roxanna Ramirez was working in the loss prevention department at a Target store in the San Francisco Bay area when she noticed a man who stood out. Afterwards she said, "Something just didn't seem right. He was acting weird, as if he was up to something." Even though the man didn't steal anything, his behavior piqued her interest and she intuitively recognized him as an anomaly. Using the store's video surveillance system, she tracked the man out to his car, where he began shaking the steering wheel. While there was nothing she could do or needed to do at that moment, she wrote down the man's license plate number. A few hours later she learned about an Amber Alert for a seven-year-old girl and thought that the make and model of the abductor's car was similar to the man she followed through Target. She called in a tip. That tip led to the arrest of David Allen Douglas and the safe recovery of a missing girl who was sitting in the back of his car.[181] Ms. Ramirez's awareness helped save a girl's life. Because she had been operating in Condition Yellow and was actively searching for people who stood out from the baseline, she stopped a child abductor.

Getting left of bang requires identifying a potential threat before something happens. That "something" could be an attack, abduction, or even a robbery. The key is to observe pre-event indicators, and to do this it is necessary to be in Condition Yellow: aware and observant. However, it is also necessary to move beyond simply observing pre-event indicators and concluding that something may happen. Effectively operating left of bang requires taking action.

This only happens if you are able to transition from Condition Yellow into Condition Orange and then Condition Red.

Because nonverbal behavior makes up between 60 percent and 90 percent of everything that humans communicate, trying to identify potential threats without knowledge of the six domains will be extremely difficult. Some of the examples we have referred to throughout the book are about average folks who, without knowledge of the six domains, were able to operate left of bang and stop potentially disastrous events without having any training in combat profiling. However, their observations were based either on years of experience or a vague gut feeling. Experience is an incredible tool to use—the problem is it takes years to build. Without explicitly knowing how to look for behavioral pre-event indicators, most Marines, soldiers, police officers, security guards or others trying to ensure their own safety would have to wait for an event to happen to know something is wrong. This is right of bang. This is reactive. This doesn't have to happen.

The six domains of behavior can be explicitly used to establish a baseline and hunt for anomalies. They give the "Marine on the ground" tangible things to look for and assess. Combat profiling will not remove all the uncertainty that exists in a situation, but it can help Marines focus on the important information and use that to make better decisions.

In 2011, one of our Combat Hunter instructors was transferred to an infantry unit, based out of Camp Pendleton, CA, that was scheduled to deploy to Afghanistan. After joining his new battalion, he was assigned as a section leader in the Combined Anti-Armor Team (CAAT) platoon. He immediately began training his Marines in the skills of Combat Hunter (combat tracking, combat profiling, and observation), on top of the numerous required skills that his

Marines needed to learn (weaponry, tactics, standard operating procedures, communication, patrolling, etc.). Throughout the deployment, he and his Marines used combat profiling and the other Combat Hunter skills with great success. By establishing the behavioral baseline of his area of operation (AO), observing human behavior and identifying anomalies, his CAAT section was incredibly successful at reducing Taliban influence, positively influencing the local populace, and hindering the Taliban's ability to operate in the area. Additionally, by employing the principles of tracking as well as establishing baselines and looking for anomalies in the physical environment, he and his Marines spotted numerous improvised explosive devices (IEDs) before the insurgents were able to detonate them. Not one IED detonated on his CAAT section.

After he returned from his deployment, we interviewed him to see how combat profiling helped him and his Marines "in country." This is a part of his response:*

It wasn't about getting the big wins. For us, combat profiling didn't provide us with one big knockout victory, but it provided countless small wins throughout the course of our deployment. When we first arrived in the area, the local villagers hated us. We would try to start conversations with them only to watch them turn their backs on us or yell at us to go away. They would say, "Go away, you'll get my family killed." We weren't making much progress.

Being a mobile unit, we were moved around a lot and weren't always in the same area, which meant we had to constantly work hard to establish a baseline and ensure that we could figure out what was going on in the areas we just arrived in. We began to look at our AO for habitual areas and anchor points. We went where the people were; while other units tried to stay away from those places. Going where the people were often kept us from getting blown up. We established baselines just by observing behavior. We asked, "What do people in this area

* We have purposely kept the report of this interview anonymous to maintain the Marine's privacy. He is currently a Staff Sergeant serving at Marine Corps Base Quantico, VA.

do, day in and day out?" And establishing a baseline was about more than just human behavior. Literally, everything in an area is part of the baseline. We were able to identify the signals that the Taliban was using to track our patrol and communicate with one another, just by observing anomalies in the area.

We found that in each area we went to, we could figure out who the key leaders were simply by observing behavior. Once we were able to identify and talk with the leaders in each of the villages, the locals' attitude toward us quickly changed. There was one guy who we all thought was the "village idiot." He didn't work and just seemed to bum around all day. We didn't realize that he was the one in charge. He didn't work because he didn't have to. But after observing him for a while, we noticed that people were constantly coming to him. You see, at first, we thought the key leaders were the oldest males—the senior village elders. We thought the leaders were the ones who were the most vocal, who seemed to speak on behalf of the village. But this was just a front. After observing people's behavior we began to notice something—that when we were talking to a group of people, certain people would step back. We began to identify the key leaders because their behavior was always a little different than the rest of the people. Sometimes the leader would be the person in the group who wouldn't talk to us at all. We realized that it wasn't the people who were talking to us that were in charge, but the one or two people present who weren't talking to us. Their silence was an anomaly. They were letting their subordinates do the talking for them. We also noticed that the true leaders may not have been verbally responding to the conversations, but they were physically responding. Sometimes it was a change in their facial expressions, sometimes they were physically drawn closer to the conversation, and sometimes it was a clear shift in their body language. And even though they were trying hard to appear uninterested, their behavior gave them away.

Once we identified that the "quiet" ones were the potential leaders, we began to observe where they lived. As we watched some of these individuals further, we would notice people coming and going from their houses at all hours of the day, and in much higher frequency than other houses. We determined their houses were anchor points. So we worked hard to establish a relationship with these people who we thought might be leaders. As we did, we watched the town and our *baseline start to change. People began to open up—they became less dominant and uncomfortable in our presence. They would invite us into their houses and even approach our patrol base to talk to us. They weren't afraid of being seen by the Taliban talking to us. They started providing us with information, letting us know where weapons were being hidden and when attacks were planned. As they became more comfortable around us, that became our new baseline. It was all because the person they viewed as the leader had accepted us and was working with us. They were just following suit.*

As the locals began to support us more, we noticed that the IEDs were being placed further and further from the village. We saw the villages literally becoming safer to patrol. Being aware of people's behavior helped us to achieve these small victories because we could identify who had the influence over the rest of the villagers.

As the local people became more comfortable around us, it also became easier to recognize those who stood out. When we saw people who were clearly uncomfortable in our presence it would tell us one of two things. Either they were uncomfortable because they were hiding something in their houses or compounds (usually they were Taliban themselves or were Taliban supporters), or they were being watched by the Taliban and were afraid of the consequences if they were seen talking to us. By observing behavior, we were able to find the insurgents hiding in plain sight. This also led to finding more weapon caches. Between these small wins and using the combat profiling terminology to communicate with adjacent units and in after action reports, we were able to learn what other units were doing successfully and incorporate that into our operations. But it all started by having a common understanding of human behavior, and what the behavior of the villagers communicated. We used combat profiling every single day that we were around the Afghan people. It kept us alive.

This Marine and his CAAT section used combat profiling on a daily basis to stay alive, influence the villagers they interacted with, identify who were the insurgents or insurgent sympathizers, and locate weapons caches and IEDs. They were able to recognize the behaviors that stood out from the baseline. They were able to identify the true leaders and use that information to their advantage. They saw noticeable and significant shifts in locals' attitudes toward the Marines, which resulted in the villages becoming safer places for the Marines to operate. Taliban influence waned. Marines stayed alive.

The six domains of behavior are different lenses to look through to understand the environment and people in a way that most people have never previously considered. When you begin looking at situations through the lenses of the six domains, you develop better situational awareness and are more likely to pick up on other people's intentions so that you can proactively respond. Many of the behaviors that make up the domains are likely not new to most readers. And almost everyone has recognized someone who has stood out from the crowd. However, most people don't do anything about what they observe and are caught *reacting* to a crisis. By employing the principles of combat profiling, you will be better able to observe pre-event indicators, identify that a crisis may occur, and *do something about it*.

Throughout the book, we've talked about different examples of when members of the military or law enforcement have recognized something was wrong, but the applications of these behaviors go well beyond the battlefield overseas or gang controlled neighborhoods of LA. The six domains of behavior can be observed everywhere we go. As the story of Ms. Ramirez shows, oftentimes it is more important to be aware when you're close to home and where you are likely to feel the safest. Every situation is going to be a little different and the lens that you use to get left of bang might change, but being left of bang is all about being able to understand the people around you and how their actions indicate their intentions.

2. APPLYING PROFILING

"It isn't just the benefit of establishing a baseline that you gain by going through the process; the increased understanding of everyone involved is the real accomplishment. This is what will make Marines more adaptable. This is what will make them better hunters. This is what will make them more survivable."
— U.S. Marine who has attended a Combat Hunter course

Feedback From the Frontlines

Following their very successful deployment to Afghanistan from the end of 2010 and into 2011, we had the opportunity to sit down with a group of Noncommissioned Officers and Officers from 2nd Battalion, 1st Marines, to get feedback on how Combat Hunter helped them while deployed. The goal was to see if there were any gaps in the Combat Hunter course that we could adjust to provide the greatest support for Marines overseas. We came away from the interview very impressed with the Marines' ability to apply what they had learned in their training to the situations they encountered in Afghanistan.

That group of Marines agreed that it would take a squad of Marines (thirteen Marines) approximately fifteen patrols before they could establish a baseline for the village in which they were operating. This is through no fault of their own. Marines are trained to continually vary their routes to prevent setting patterns, so during those fifteen patrols, the Marines were not necessarily exposed to the same areas every time. If that squad was one of three squads at a platoon-sized patrol base, then Marines were being exposed to the local populace and enemy almost forty-five times before they felt they really understood the area they were responsible for controlling.

These Marines were developing their implicit understanding of that area, but their ability to establish a baseline was hindered because developing tacit knowledge takes time. Without having a baseline to compare their observations to, their ability to identify threats and identify people who didn't fit in was greatly reduced during those initial few weeks in Afghanistan. The other reason that this raised a concern for us is that the enemy was able to observe the Marines on forty-five occasions, developing their knowledge of the Marines and identifying their patterns. Additionally, it wasn't only the enemy that was observing the Marines, but the entire village.

This interview began the initiative to develop a systematic approach to establishing a baseline to shorten the time required to have a functioning understanding of an area at the beginning of a deployment. The added benefit to this is that Marines can patrol and operate with an explicit understanding of what to look for to more effectively and quickly establish a baseline. Over time, the explicit knowledge that is created on the first few patrols will become implicit and will expand past the results of the first attempts. The immediate goal is to find quantifiable observations that can be communicated across a unit and reduce the continuous exposure needed to create a mutual understanding of an area's baseline.[182]

The method we advocate for developing your ability to explicitly establish baselines and applying the combat profiling method is a three-step approach. By consistently and explicitly going through this process, you will quicken your ability to understand your surroundings, speed up your ability to identify anomalies, and ultimately increase your decision-making abilities. The more you use this process, the quicker you'll begin to tacitly evaluate your environment and the less mental energy you'll require to establish baselines and identify anomalies.

The three steps can be summed up with a few simple questions: First, what is going on here? Second, what would cause someone to stand out and why? Third, what would I do about it? The key to combat profiling is understanding the behavioral patterns of an area and individuals (establish the baseline) and then identifying those individuals or situations that break the patterns (find the anomalies).

What is going on here?

The first step begins by making a quick and immediate assessment about the atmospherics of the area. At first glance, does the area have positive or negative atmospherics? If the area has positive atmospherics, is there anyone whose attitude or behavioral cluster doesn't fit the baseline? This person may warrant a second look. If the area has negative atmospherics, is there anyone in the area who is displaying the comfortable cluster? This first step is designed to quickly determine if there is anyone blatantly deviating from the baseline. The key questions are:

- What is the general feel of the place? What is the common emotion? Is it positive or negative? What are the common or consistent behaviors among people in the area? Are people comfortable, uncomfortable, relaxed, aggressive, etc.?
- What defines this situation: order/disorder, busy/ slow, crowded/uncrowded?

The second element of understanding "what is going on here?" is to determine the type of place you're in based on geographics and iconography. Geographics defines the large-scale patterns of an environment or situation. Iconography provides further atmospheric indicators and gives you a sense of the groups and messages affiliated with the area. Atmospherics and proxemics help to interpret the geographic behaviors. The key questions are:

- Where am I? Am I in (or observing) a habitual area or an anchor point?
- Are there anchor points within the habitual area? Who controls them? What behaviors or indicators identify the anchor points? Are there people providing over-watch or physical security? Are there passive security measures (e.g., cameras, fences)? Are most people avoiding a specific location, while only certain people are proxemically pulled to that location?
- What are the natural lines of drift? Where are people headed?

Ultimately, the combat profiler is attempting to determine the large-scale behavioral patterns in order to establish a standard against which to judge anomalies. As the combat profiler asks and answers these questions, he or she should also attempt to identify the underlying cause for the observed behaviors: e.g., why is the place crowded? Why are people keeping a certain distance from one another? Why is the atmosphere positive or negative?

Finally, the third part of answering the question of "what is going on here?" is to understand the behavioral patterns that are occurring and identify the processes that are unique to the area you are observing. This third step takes the observations down to the micro-level and is focused on individuals and groups of people. The key questions are:

- What patterns of movement do I observe? Are people being proxemically pulled toward or pushed away from someone or something?
- What distance are people keeping from one another?
- What activities do I observe?

While working through this first step, the combat profiler should not disregard appropriate assumptions in helping to judge the observations being made. We believe it is important to use the knowledge of parallel situations from other contexts to develop reasonable assumptions for what types of behavior to expect. For example, while a market in downtown Los Angeles will look different and have different behaviors present than a bazaar in the Middle East, similarities in behavioral patterns will still exist. This is due to shared human nature which restricts and encourages similar types of behaviors in the two situations. Trading, selling, bargaining patterns caused by proxemic necessities and spatial organization, and various other elements, create numerous similarities between a U.S. market and a Middle Eastern bazaar. Forming useful and effective analogies is key for combat profilers. They provide the combat profiler with initial sets of expectations and assumptions that can be quickly confirmed. These assumptions will sometimes need to be corrected, but they speed up the observational process and are better than starting from scratch.

Almost all aspects of human behavior can be potential elements of a baseline: when people get up, when locals visit the marketplace, when people go to sleep, traffic patterns, greeting behaviors, and numerous other behaviors. It is important that combat profilers are explicit about what types of behaviors they are using to establish the baseline for the area and ensure that they record their observations. Combat profilers should also consistently update baseline observations as behaviors shift and change overtime.

What would cause someone to stand out and why?

The second step moves the combat profiler toward more focused and specific observations, with the distinct goal of being prepared to identify anomalies. While the first step provides the combat profiler with a picture of the "norm," during step two, the combat profiler focuses his or her observations on those things that would go above and below the norm—the things that don't fit the situation. Here, the domains that are of most help are proxemics, kinesics, biometrics, and iconography. Proxemics helps to identify unusual movement and placement of individuals. Kinesics and biometrics help to identify those whose emotions, attitudes, and intentions do not fit the normal emotions, attitudes, and behavior of the situation. Iconography will help to identify affiliations, motivations, and messages. The goal is to begin mentally preparing to identify the person who stands out. The key questions to ask during this step include:

- Who seems familiar or unfamiliar with the area?
- Who has access to anchor points? What is the clothing and behavior of those individuals?
- Who appears uncomfortable, dominant, interested or uninterested?
- Whose movement appears aggressive? Who is proxemically too close, or pushed too far away?
- Whose behavior appears unnatural or distracted? Whose attention appears divided?
- Whose iconography associates them with hostile or threatening causes? Which individuals in the crowd may be affiliated with one another based on similar iconography?
- Is anyone exhibiting smuggling behavior or checking his or her "six"?
- Does anyone's biometric cues indicate distress, discomfort, anger, anxiety, or other negative emotions?

What would I do about it?

The third step is simply to think about the action you would take based on your observations. This is the application of the combat profiling heuristic. The first question: is anyone an obvious hostile threat? If so, what is your plan to deal with it? If not, then is anyone giving off three (or more) behavioral indicators that they are an anomaly? Remember, when you observe three indicators, you have to act! Decide which type of behaviors would warrant different responses. Action may simply be contacting the person to ask some questions and observing them up close. But do not wait until further indicators are exhibited because it may be too late. Based on the combat profiling heuristic, you must do something. For the Marine in a combat environment, the decisions are kill, capture, or contact. For the civilian in a potentially unsafe situation, the decisions are run, hide, or fight. Each situation will be different. A security agent in a public transportation facility may decide that their hierarchy of decisions is question, detain, or subdue. A civilian in the same location might consider report, alert (i.e., sound an alarm), or run. A police officer on patrol may have to decide between shoot, arrest, or question. Regardless of what situation you find yourself in, or what role you are playing at the moment, you must have a set of pre-established decisions to make based on what you observe. Otherwise, you'll freeze, take too long, or make a decision that is not in your best interest.

These three steps are a basic guide to establishing a baseline, thinking about how you will identify anomalies, and being ready to act quickly. This is for your safety and that of others. Following these steps will keep you left of bang.

3. ESTABLISHING BASELINES EVERYWHERE YOU GO

As discussed above, when arriving in a new area, the first task is to determine what is going on in the area you are operating in/observing: the geographic and behavioral patterns. Although each setting is unique, the general approach discussed above will help in establishing baselines for every place a Marine might encounter while deployed. However, there is another way that a Marine can shorten the time needed to go through that process, and that is by finding similar locations here in the states with which to draw analogies to places overseas.

If a Marine unit expects to conduct a high number of vehicle or personnel checkpoints, there are a number of places to practice establishing a baseline. A person could observe the behavior of people standing in line at a department of motor vehicles, at a TSA checkpoint at an airport, or even a border-crossing checkpoint. By initially analyzing the behavior of the people at the checkpoint, observing each domain one at a time, and then analyzing behavior encompassing all of the domains, Marines can quickly establish a baseline for that setting. The more experience combat profilers have at analyzing people and places using the Six Domains, the larger file folders they will create and the quicker they will be able to make observations in new environments. This is particularly true if combat profilers can observe situations at home that mirror or provide analogies to situations abroad. If a unit expects to be operating in a mostly rural area, Marines could observe the behavior of people who work in similar industries. There could be a great number of similarities between the behavior of a field worker in the U.S. and a farmer overseas.

Combat profilers may not be able to find parallel experiences at home for some situations that they will face overseas, such as IED attacks. In situations like these, Marines and soldiers need the ability to conduct a mental simulation[183] of what they would expect to be the baseline for the event. This will dramatically reduce the time needed to make sense of what is occurring when they arrive at a chaotic scene. The high degree of uncertainty and the element of the unknown can cause stress that limits your ability to think clearly in these scenarios. Taking the time before you deploy to list any possible contingencies you may respond to and discussing them with people who have experienced similar events on previous deployments can help you to build templates for those contingencies.

The picture below depicts the scene around a gang shooting victim in Los Angeles.

(Photo Courtesy of Brandon Valdez)

To establish an immediate baseline for this event, it is safe to assume that the deceased victim would become a center of focus for the surrounding people. However, only people who are familiar with victims or who have an interest in them would approach them (proxemic pull). These people may be first responders who want to provide first aid and save the person's life. They could also be people who want to remove things from the body (either something that they own and want to get back or to steal something that they want from the victim) before the police arrive. With the exception of those two groups of people, we would expect all of the other bystanders to be proxemically pushed away from the victim, as they would have no need to get any closer.

We would expect people who had no warning that these two men were going to be killed to be shocked at the event, causing them to display a cluster of uncomfortable behaviors, while someone who anticipated the event may show a lower degree of interest in the scene because they saw it coming. We would also expect people to be showing a submissive cluster in response to the scene as they realize that two people are now dead. The other extreme of this situation would be people who are so angered by the event that they display dominance as they become emotionally aroused and experience a rush of adrenaline.

With these very basic assumptions formed for a baseline, we may consider the Los Angeles picture by first looking at the girl on the right edge of the photo.* Her body language shows that she is interested in the scene: her feet, torso, and gaze are all directly oriented at the victims. We could conclude that she is feeling uncomfortable, since she is

---

* For any picture that is analyzed, we accept that the photo is a moment in time and may not reflect the true behavior the person is displaying. Pictures are chosen for the instructional value that they provide. More accurate conclusions could be made with video footage or additional pictures of the person or situation.

displaying pacifying behaviors as she rubs her clavicle and has crossed her arms across her chest. These observations fit our initial assumptions, leading toward the decision that she fits the baseline and does not warrant any additional attention at the moment. Shifting left in the picture and observing the female wearing a white sweatshirt and Capri pants, we come to a similar conclusion as the first female. She has covered her mouth with her hand, which is a response often associated with surprise and grief.* Since she also fits the baseline, she does not need any immediate attention.

The third female in the picture, wearing a white shirt, jeans, and white sneakers, however, is an anomaly and does not fit the baseline. First, one foot is oriented toward the scene and the other foot is pointing away from the scene, showing that she may be preparing to leave the area. Her divided interest causes her to stand out from the other two women. The other indicator is the "hands on the hip" posture, which we classify in the dominance cluster. The fact that she does not fit the baseline and stands out as an anomaly does not indicate any wrongdoing. But it requires at least contacting her to find out what information she may have about either the victims or the shooters.

Any time Marines attempt to establish a baseline using either analogy or a mental simulation approach, they will arrive on the scene with a set of assumptions. In many situations, the assumptions will initially far outweigh the facts. Because combat profilers may enter a situation with a high degree of unconfirmed assumptions, the need for accurate and actionable information is very high in order to raise their awareness about the event. The benefit of our approach is that they can quickly adjust their assumptions and fill in the gaps of information.

---

* Many pictures of the response to the September 11 attacks in New York City show onlookers with this pose, covering their mouths in shock.

We believe that there will be enough similarities between various situations in the U.S. and analogous situations overseas that developing initial assumptions will shorten the time required to develop a baseline while deployed. Without a baseline, you will have nothing against which to compare your observations and no way to assess initially whether or not a person is an anomaly. The intent of combat profiling is to increase a Marine's situational awareness and survivability. By practicing establishing baselines now, you can decrease the time needed to isolate the enemy and minimize the chance of an enemy hunting *you*.

4. IDENTIFYING KEY LEADERS

Understanding human behavior is hugely beneficial to Marines and helps them gain the upper hand in their daily lives while at home or deployed. Application of this understanding is most helpful for Marines as they attempt to identify key leaders in any group of people. While often the leader will willingly identify himself, there could be situations in which he conceals his role. Often, combat profilers must observe from a distance and will not have the benefits of being introduced to the key leader. How, then, can key leaders be identified? Human behavior and group dynamics are key.

In relation to combat, in highly kinetic scenarios, a sniper team capable of identifying a leader from a thousand yards away with a high degree of certainty can provide several options to the ground commander: they can kill that leader, maneuver ground forces to detain the leader, or continue observation to gain more information. In counterinsurgency situations where there is a greater need to influence the local population as a means of gaining intelligence to root out insurgents, identifying the local leaders and power brokers in a village is critical. The key-leader indicators discussed here are not limited solely to enemy leaders, but any leader within a group of people.

The MADE Man

In the Italian Mafia, becoming a "made" man is associated with status, respect, and a higher-level power in the organization's hierarchy. To help Marines remember the four main behavioral indicators for leaders, we use the acronym MADE. These indicators are Mimicry, Adoration, Direction, and Entourage.* Anytime you observe these elements of behavior, you can be reasonably certain you have identified the leader of the group.

Entourage

The first indicator for identifying key leaders is an entourage. In fact, it's a necessary indicator, since it's difficult to identify a key leader of a group without a group. An entourage is simply one or more people around the leader. This may seem obvious because the well-established fact in leadership research is that interaction is one of the main activities of leaders. While the leader needs others around to control or give guidance, having an entourage comes with additional requirements. An entourage, which may include a messenger, a bodyguard, or a trusted advisor, provides a benefit to the leader. The President of the United States has an entourage made up of the Secret Service to protect him, a group of advisors to provide counsel, and support personnel who handle any task he needs done. Everyone around him provides a benefit to him because he is the leader of that group. Even though leaders will not always have as extensive

---

* Although we use the acronym MADE, we'll discuss the elements in the order EDAM, which is a more natural order for how these indicators will be observed. EDAM just doesn't make a good acronym!

an entourage as the President, an entourage will still be present.

The leader must also provide a benefit to their entourage. Whether it is money, guidance, drug connections, or protection from authorities or rivals, some reason exists for the entourage to choose and support the leader. To determine the roles of individuals inside of a group, answering questions about who is providing physical protection for whom and who is the center of attention can facilitate this effort.

Direction

The second leadership indicator is direction—the leader provides direction for the rest of the group. A leader who is significant will be in control of his subordinates. Giving direction is often a kinesic indicator designed to control the actions and behaviors of others and could either be very obvious or very subtle. Military commanders often evoke the image of giving obvious direction as they order their different units to push forward, hold firm, or any other action they require.* While obvious indicators of direction are easy to identify, such as pointing or motioning, combat profilers must also look for subtle indicators of direction. Subtle indicators could be a nod, a wink, stroking a beard, or something that would not attract much attention yet would still convey specific guidance to others.

Often times, junior leaders in an organization are easier to identify than their superiors because the junior leaders are more apt to give very obvious direction. In an attempt to exert control or make a name for themselves, they will very likely be more overt in their actions, very clearly ordering their subordinates to take certain actions. They are more likely to be offended if their orders are disobeyed. Senior

---

* If you don't have experience in the military, think of the body language that a traffic cop would use to control cars as they pass through an intersection.

leaders who have progressed through the ranks and are usually more mature may not feel the need to continuously display overt dominance. They may feel more secure in their position or do not want to attract the attention of others, which in a criminal enterprise may result in detention or arrest. Subtle indicators of direction may be more indicative of the true shot-callers.

As the human eye is naturally attracted to movement, kinesic cues associated with direction are often what will initially capture our attention and allow us to identify other leadership indicators through sustained observation.

Adoration

Adoration is the third key-leader indicator and can be defined by positive displays of admiration and respect toward an individual. These can be verbal and nonverbal, as well as overt and subtle. Verbal adoration includes language of respect. This can be calling someone "sir" or "ma'am," addressing a person by title (such as military rank, "doctor," etc.), or using formal language reserved for people of higher status (as in languages such as Korean). Nonverbal adoration encompasses actions and gestures which show deference toward another person. Overt signs of adoration include gestures such as saluting, bowing, or kissing the hand. Subtle signs of adoration include things such as walking behind the person of higher rank, holding the door open, standing in a posture of submissiveness, physically sitting at a lower height than the key leader, standing while the key leader sits, looking to the key leader for acknowledgement, etc.* In many situations, criminals or even locals who are friendly toward us will not want to overtly indicate who their key leader is. It is fairly easy to temporarily refrain from showing overt signs of adoration; however, it is very difficult to keep from showing subtle signs of adoration toward a superior because they are so ingrained in people's behavior. Behavior will betray intentions and relationships— with sustained observation combat profilers can confidently identify the key leaders and decision makers in any group.

Mimicry

The last leadership indicator is mimicry which includes the subconscious gestures, mannerisms, facial expressions, postures, speech patterns, accents, and other behaviors that people display which are identical to those they are interacting with.[184] Research has shown that mimicry is a positive element of group dynamics that establishes rapport and increases positive relationships between group members.

Mimicry was even a method employed by our ancestors to survive because, in the harsh conditions in which they lived, social isolates did not survive.[185] Mimicking another person's actions demonstrates respect, and often people subconsciously and naturally mimic those whom they respect. While behavioral mimicry can be a deliberate act and done intentionally, also important are the elements of mimicry that occur outside of conscious awareness. These are true

---

* An example of overt and subtle adoration can be seen in a Taliban video that shows Taliban fighters looting a base from which U.S. forces had withdrawn (in Kamdesh, Afghanistan). For the video go to www.cp-journal.com/leftofbang, and view the post labeled "Finding the Leader—Adoration." At about the four-minute, 40-second mark, a truck drives into the compound, and several individuals get out. One of the individuals is wearing light brown clothes with a dark brown vest and is carrying a rifle in his left hand. Soon, all of the Taliban fighters gather around this man and proceed to line up to shake his hand and greet him (overt adoration). However, if you look closely, a subtle form of adoration occurs when what appears to be his "right-hand man" discreetly takes the rifle from the leader so that he can shake hands and hug the fighters.

indicators of social standing and authority. Because people show a higher degree of mimicry when they are interacting with others by whom they want to be accepted,[186] combat profilers should look for the person who initiates a specific behavior as well as the people who match or mimic that behavior. The leader will often be the dominant person in the group and therefore the one who first assumes a posture, expression, or gesture which is subsequently mimicked by the rest of the group.*

When done outside of conscious awareness, mimicry will show where a person's true respect lies and may not always sync with an accepted hierarchy in an organization. Many companies, militaries, and social groups have a person who has been chosen to be the public and visible leader, while there is a strong-willed second in command who is the glue in the organization and has earned the trust and respect of those with whom they work. Subtle displays of mimicry will help you find who the real leaders are in any group.

Finding the MADE Man

In situations where you can observe four out of four, or even three out of four, indicators previously discussed, you can be reasonably certain that you are watching the leader of the group. Other times, you may be alerted to the presence of a leader based on other aspects of the profiling domains, and the preceding indicators can be used to supplement your observations. As each situation you find yourself in will be slightly different, these indicators may help you identify the leaders in the groups you are observing. Finding and targeting these people can not only improve your effectiveness but also improve the perception of your capabilities.

---

* Mimicry is not inevitable between people, and there will be times when "counter-mimicry" is used by people who take deliberate action not to mimic the behavior of those surrounding them.

Counterinsurgencies can turn into a "war of information," and those with the most influence can greatly affect the outcome. Finding those people with influence is a significant way to tip the scales in your favor.

5. STAYING LEFT OF BANG: ATTACKS FROM WITHIN[187]

"Workplace violence," "insider threat," or "green-on-blue attack." Call it what you will but the reality remains the same. Those who we are supposed to be able to trust violate that very trust by conducting a violent attack against their own. For U.S. military personnel, the threat of "green-on-blue" attacks has risen considerably in the past few years. According to one ongoing database, green-on-blue attacks (attacks against coalition personnel by members of joint security forces) more than tripled from 2010 to 2011. The most attacks occurred in 2012, with approximately 44 separate incidents resulting in 61 coalition deaths. From January 2008 until October 2013, there were approximately 85 green-on-blue attacks resulting in around 140 killed and 159 wounded coalition personnel.[188]

The reason for this increase in attacks by Afghan security force personnel is largely due to the heightened risk resulting from the increase in joint operations (such as patrols) and the increased mentorship roles that coalition forces have assumed. More interpersonal interaction results in a greater risk. The causes of these attacks mainly fall into two categories. First, tensions resulting from cultural differences and interpersonal conflict. Second, infiltration and influence by insurgent groups. In August 2013, the International Security and Assistance Force Commander, General John Allen stated that up to 25 percent of green-on-blue attacks were the result of insurgent infiltration; however, the majority were the result of personal grievances.[189] As long as Marines and other U.S. military personnel continue to work alongside host-nation security forces, the threat of these types of attacks will remain. The key is to take the necessary steps to mitigate these attacks and train our own security forces to stay left of bang.

The problem of green-on-blue attacks presents a very complex scenario for the military, as the mission in Afghanistan is to train and develop the Afghan National Security Forces (ANSF) so that they can take charge of their own national security. This is a mission that requires well-developed relationships between the soldiers of each country and a high level of trust between mentor and mentee. If the American military treats every Afghan soldier as a potential threat, taking away their ammunition, searching them at checkpoints, and treating them as second-class citizens, these relationships will be destroyed and the mission will fail. On the other hand, the ANSF can't be treated as harmless, and the military can't completely let their guard down. That approach would expose our forces to an unacceptable level of risk, and would likewise cause the mission to fail. Because the impact of green-on-blue incidents strains this relationship and jeopardizes over eleven years of combat, "threats inside the wire" have attracted the attention at the highest levels of the military and government.

In addition to green-on-blue attacks, our forces have occasionally been the victims of deliberate "blue-on-blue" violence. Usually the phrase blue-on-blue is used to refer to incidents in which U.S. personnel fire upon other U.S. personnel whether by accident or through negligence. At times, however, blue-on-blue violence is the result of a U.S. service member, contractor, or government employee attacking other U.S. personnel because of deliberate and malicious intent. One of the highest profile examples in recent times has been the case of Major Nidal Hasan (U.S. Army), who killed 13 people and injured more than 30 others at Fort Hood in 2009. More recently in September 2013, Navy contractor Aaron Alexis shot 15 people with a shotgun, killing 12 of them, after entering the Washington Navy Yard with a valid ID card. Since these are not the only examples of this type of attack, the insider threat is always a risk that needs to be considered.

The American military is not alone in experiencing workplace violence or insider attacks. A 2001 report estimated that 1.7 million "violent victimizations" occurred in U.S. workplaces between 1993 and 1999. Seventy-five percent of these were simple assaults; although less than 1 percent were homicides.[190] An entire industry exists to provide training, advice, and security assistance to prevent and respond to workplace violence. Additionally, we have become increasingly aware of events such as school shootings and other types of attacks in places we previously thought were (relatively) safe. On one hand, these types of attacks are a part of the larger issues of crime we face in the U.S. According to the FBI's Uniform Crime Reporting Program, there were approximately 1,214,462 violent crimes nationwide in 2012.[191] On the other hand, issues such as workplace violence and school shootings seem more threatening, more unbelievable, perhaps because they occur in places where we should be able to trust that our children and we are safe. In many ways, workplace violence and school shootings parallel the green-on-blue and malicious blue-on-blue attacks our military personnel experience here and overseas.

Various studies have defined civilian workplace violence by four main categories:[192]

- Civilian Type 1: These include violent acts by criminals who are unconnected with the workplace. These are acts such as robberies.
- Civilian Type 2: These include violence directed toward employees by customers, clients, or others that the organization provides services for.
- Civilian Type 3: This is defined as violence against employees by other current or former employees.
- Civilian Type 4: These are violence acts committed in the workplace by someone who doesn't work there, but who has a personal relationship to an employee (e.g., a spouse or partner).

From the perspective of deployed military forces, we may disregard the "Type 4" incidents for several reasons. However, Types 1-3 relate to the types of violence that our military forces experience, which can also be broken up into four categories:

- Military Type 1: Violent acts by insurgents and other hostile forces against U.S. patrols or bases (e.g., patrol bases or forward operating bases). (Civilian Type 1)
- Military Type 2: Violent acts by locals who are not a part of an insurgent group. (Civilian Type 2)
- Military Type 3: Violent acts by assumed coalition personnel (i.e., green-on-blue). (Civilian Type 3)
- Military Type 4: Violent acts by fellow U.S. personnel (i.e., malicious blue-on-blue; e.g., Maj Hasan). (Civilian Type 3)

The Military Type 1 events equate to traditional attacks against U.S. forces by insurgents and other hostile forces. But these are expected. The usual training, precautions, and security measures apply to deny the enemy the ability to conduct these attacks. Offensive tactics, such as dispersion, 360-degree security, and over-watch, help to mitigate some of the risks of these types of attacks. Defensive obstacles, checkpoints and barricades, security positions, and other measures help to create defensive standoffs to keep hostile forces out of our positions. However, these types of risks come with the job, and it's combating these types of attacks that our military personnel are best trained to deal with.

The Military Type 2 are those in which local civilians, who are not active members of a hostile or insurgent group, attack U.S. or coalition forces. These are often the result of grievances, such as the loss of a child or other family member. Civilian casualties are an ugly reality of violent conflict and often fuel negative sentiment against militaries and other security forces operating in the area. These attacks may be spontaneous or premeditated. In the types of environments in which U.S. forces are currently operating, it is extremely difficult to distinguish between these types of attacks and Military Type 1 attacks which involve recognized enemy forces. The same types of tactics and defensive measures help to mitigate the effects of these attacks. Nevertheless, it is critically important that we attempt to minimize civilian casualties and treat local civilians with respect. Insurgencies, and even policing missions, require the support of the local populace.

The two types of attacks that are defined as insider attacks are Types 3 and 4. These are violent acts conducted against our own forces by the people we should be able to trust the most: fellow coalition partners and even our own military and defense personnel. Until recently, these types of attacks had been relatively rare, although not unknown. Our military personnel need training to be able to prevent these acts from happening. Combat profiling can provide a number of tools to stay left-of-bang.

Combat profiling gives Marines and other military personnel three tools to help prevent insider attacks: the proactive, combat hunter mindset; the ability to identify pre-event indicators; and the ability to make quick and accurate decisions with little time and little information.

Combat Hunter Mindset

The FBI suggests that one way to survive workplace violence is having a "survival mindset." This means being aware, prepared, and having rehearsed the actions you will take during a workplace violence incident.[193] Those who prepare and train themselves for the possibility of violence will react differently than those who do not. Those who are not prepared will likely panic and will ultimately become helpless (Condition Black). Those who are prepared will still experience anxiety but will be more likely to maintain awareness and act effectively in a stressful situation (possibly going as far as Condition Red). Rather than a "survival mindset," we recommend that you have a "combat hunter" mindset. The first element of this mindset is maintaining a Condition Yellow awareness level. It means maintaining your situational awareness.

The reality is, however, that it is not always possible to be in Condition Yellow 100 percent of the time. When a person focuses on reading an account report, is engaged in an important business related conversation, or conducts a number of other tasks, that person's situational awareness will be limited, or possibly even lost. However, there is no excuse for walking around the entire day completely unaware of your surroundings. After reading a report or finishing a task or conversation, everyone should assess his or her surroundings. This may only take a few seconds but may be the difference between being a victim and being a survivor. For Marines and other deployed service members, it is also not possible for every single individual to be completely aware and searching for threats at all times. However, they have an advantage in that Marines and soldiers can be assigned to serve as "guardian angels." These are personnel whose job it is to be on the lookout, at all times, for potential threats. Additionally, military forces can establish and maintain various security measures not available to many civilian organizations, such as security checkpoints and personnel searches. This means that military bases abroad are very controlled environments. And, instead of letting this lead to complacence, Marines and other security personnel should recognize that the security measures in place provide for an even greater ability to identify potential threats and prevent attacks.

Identify Pre-Event Indicators

Attacks do not happen "out of the blue." Even what may be considered spontaneous violence is almost always the result of a gradual progression of aggression and pre-cursors to violence. In order to conduct attacks, terrorist groups must plan, prepare, reconnoiter, rehearse, stage for the attack, move to the location of the attack, and numerous other things before actually conducting the attack. The same can be said about the workplace shooter, the rapist, or the violent assaulter. However, as the FBI states, "It must be pointed out, however, that no single behavior is more suggestive of violence than another. All actions have to be judged in the proper context and in totality to determine the potential for violence."[194] Nevertheless, the key to preventing many attacks is identifying the pre-event indicators.

Combat profiling focuses on observing behavioral indicators that someone is a potential threat. These include autonomic indicators of emotions and stress (biometric cues), behavioral indicators of aggression (kinesics), violations of interpersonal distance and other movements that attackers make (proxemics), and various other behavior clues that a person wants to do another person harm. Military personnel, or anyone in a workplace, should look for these and other indicators that someone may be planning or preparing to conduct an insider attack.

Behavioral Indicators

Combat profiling is primarily a method of behavioral analysis—analyzing a person's behavior to determine their emotions and intentions. We expect to see similar type behaviors from someone who is planning to conduct an attack.

- Nervous behaviors (uncomfortable cluster) – Personally and physically conducting an attack against another person requires a great deal of risk. The attacker is at personal risk at a number of points from initial planning to the actual attack itself. Most people will be uncomfortable with the chance of getting caught or having their attack thwarted. Drug dealers, shoplifters, smugglers, and even suicide bombers would rather not be caught. Instead, they want to accomplish their goal and carry out their mission. Additionally, people have a natural aversion to pain, injury, and death. Human nature produces a strong desire for survival, and very few (if any) people can or will walk into the face of death unaffected and undeterred—even the most idealistic suicide bomber. That being the case, anyone who seeks to accomplish a task in a situation where there is high risk of getting caught and a significant potential for injury or death will experience nervousness and fear as the survival instinct kicks in and releases a number of hormones such as adrenaline.

- Concealing the plan (uncomfortable cluster) – Prior to the actual attack, any individuals who are involved in planning the attack will likely exhibit secretive behavior. This will likely be expressed in various ways. One the one hand, a potential attacker (or any individual involved in the plan) will seek to hide the fact that an attack is being planned and prepared for. This may result in avoidance behaviors or proxemic pushes away from those who might be able to intervene and prevent the attack. On the other hand, a potential attacker may also exhibit aggressive behaviors as a counterresponse to those inquiring about the secretive behavior. In these cases, the person may exhibit a behavioral cluster shift from uncomfortable to dominant behaviors. Both of these types of behavior will likely be outside of the normal behavioral baseline for any given person and should be reasons for suspicion and potential action.

- Interest in the target – An attacker will have to observe, learn about, and ultimately get close enough to the target for the attack to be effective. Depending upon the type of attack and weapon being used, an attacker may have to get extremely close for the attack to be successful. Suicide bombers must be within feet of the target. Over a period of time, an attacker will exhibit a consistent pattern of being proxemically pulled toward the target. The attacker's behavior will indicate interest in the target at a level that will be unnatural. At the time of attack, the attacker will move in a way that is mission focused, aggressive, and indicative of "being on the hunt." Proxemically, the attacker will move toward the target with a purpose.

Consider the analogy of a hunter or predatory animal: A hunter must acquire the prey, observe the prey, (potentially) follow the prey or wait for the prey, and eventually close in on the prey. Hunters observe their prey in order to identify patterns of behavior. Surveillance exhibits unique behavioral indicators that should be obvious to the combat profiler. The same can be said about following, or tailing. The actual attack may necessitate that the attacker close in on the target. This approach (proxemic pull) may be unusual—unusual timing, unusual speed, unusual person, and may break socially accepted proxemic rules.

PLANNING

- Acquiring, or attempting to acquire, information about security, routines, schedules, or other types of information for which the person has no reason to have.
- Accessing databases outside of their work related requirements.
- Observing individuals in an unusual manner, following certain individuals, or asking about personal matters of fellow coworkers inappropriately.
- Contacting people outside of the organization to share information.

- Behavioral indicators of increased stress and/or negative emotions toward fellow coworkers.
- Verbal or written communication that a person is thinking of doing themselves or others violence.
- Increased interest in weapons (talking about, purchasing, etc.) or violent media.
- Testing security measures.

Decision Making

Quite often, many people see one or more pre-event indicators leading up to an insider attack but fail to do anything about it. They brush it off, rationalize it, don't report it, or don't make a note of it and ultimately forget about it. This discussion is not a call to be suspicious that every coworker is plotting a major attack or to be hypervigilant to the point of distraction so that your colleagues become uncomfortable and suspicious of you. Rather, the purpose of this section is to convince you that many incidents of workplace violence and insider attacks can be prevented through people being proactive. As the saying goes, if something doesn't seem right, it probably isn't. The keys to responding well in a situation are knowing when to make a decision, knowing what decisions to make, and rehearsing those decisions so that when it comes time to act, your actions are immediate and spontaneous.

The combat profiling heuristic requires that when you observe three behavioral indicators that someone is an anomaly, you act. However, sometimes it may be necessary to act on one or two indicators, provided those indicators are clear and obvious in communicating a person is a threat.

Combat profiling also requires that you have a set of pre-determined decisions to make in the event that you observe anomalies, or pre-event indicators. For the Marine in combat, these are kill, capture, and contact. For the civilian walking about, the decisions are run, hide, and fight. For civilian workplace violence incidents, the decisions may be talk, report, and intervene: First, contact the individual, engage them in conversation, and ask probing questions to further determine if the person may actually be a threat. Second, if the conversation leads you to believe that the person is a threat, or if the indicators are clear enough, immediately report the person to the appropriate security personnel and/or authorities and provide as much detail and information as possible about why you think the person is a potential threat. Third, intervene. We would never recommend that a person purposefully put himself or herself in danger, but depending on the situation, this may be necessary. Intervention could be verbal or physical, alone or with a group. Nevertheless, the third option is chosen when a violent incident is imminent and other options are unavailable.

Combat profiling gives Marines, soldiers, other law enforcement and security personnel, as well as civilians, the mindset and knowledge to identify the behaviors and events leading up to an attack. Combat profiling increases your survivability. The combat profiling domains are uniquely designed and capable of preventing the insider attack because they train people to realize when a person has those violent intentions and provide the ability to determine if he or she is capable of carrying them out.

Preventing the Attack

We must do everything possible to prevent insider attacks. Because most insider attacks are the result of interpersonal problems, it is important that leaders take an interest in the welfare of their Marines, soldiers, and employees. Military personnel deployed abroad, and who are working closely with host-nation security forces, cannot afford to risk their own lives and the lives of their comrades by treating their host-nation counterparts disrespectfully. Preventing an attack may be as simple as respecting those we work with, treating them with dignity and like valuable members of the team, and respecting their culture and values. Unfortunately, interpersonal conflict will always arise, and violence may be the response. Additionally, some attacks are ideologically driven. In regard to Maslow's hierarchy of needs, ideology trumps every other level of human need. Even if a person has his or her basic needs taken care of, is safe, and is in an environment in which they are respected and valued, that person may still have a deep ideological problem with the organization and people around him. This is the case for people like Maj. Hasan. The only way to prevent attacks from folks like these is to establish the proper security procedures and for everyone in the organization to maintain awareness, report any pre-event indicators, and intervene if necessary.

6. DEVELOPING YOUR PROFILING ABILITY

"We evaluate people all the time, quite attentively, but they only
get our conscious attention when there is a reason. We see it all,
but we edit out most of it. Thus, when something does call out to us, we ought to
pay attention. For many people, that is a muscle they don't exercise."
—Gavin de Becker

When you first started driving a car, there were a number of different tasks that you had to simultaneously accomplish for you to successfully drive the car safely. Since you were a novice driver, your focus was internal to the car, and your attention was directed toward accomplishing all of the tasks.

The acts of using the turn signal, checking your mirrors, changing the radio, changing gears, carrying on a conversation, and turning your lights on were all independent tasks that required concentration and effort for you to accomplish separately.

It wasn't until you had spent countless hours behind the wheel that those tasks became very simple and automatic, something you simply did as part of the drive. As you became more comfortable inside the car, you also became more comfortable and aware of those who were around you on the road. You became a better judge of how much space you needed to make a left hand turn through oncoming traffic, you learned how to assess the relative speed of a car approaching in your rear view mirror, you learned the areas that highway patrol officers would likely be in to catch you speeding, and you learned the indicators that would alert you to an erratic driver that needed close attention.

The same type of development is required for you as a profiler. Early in your development, you will find yourself focusing a great deal on one single domain. You will likely be very obvious in your efforts to watch people and will likely attract attention to yourself. You will also find it difficult to profile while simultaneously being involved in a conversation. Over time and with more practice, this process will become fluid. But it takes practice and effort. The time that you put in each day to develop this ability will lead to you becoming capable of automating the tasks involved in profiling into your life the same way that you became a better driver. This will let you look farther ahead down the road and see all of the possible ways a situation could play out.

__Becoming an Expert__

The goal is to become an expert combat profiler and to be so adept at profiling that you do it intuitively. The ability to carry on a mentally taxing conversation while simultaneously analyzing the verbal and nonverbal indicators, the cues that are being presented, is reserved for the peak performers. This is a great goal to have. However, the reality of the matter is that it could take you up to ten years[195] before you reach this level of proficiency and expertise.*

I tend to believe that, to become a true expert in the field, a decade of experience could be necessary to reach the pinnacle. I also believe that there are some steps that we can take to become better profilers *today*, as well as set ourselves on a path to attain the expert level. To do this, let's take a look at what makes somebody an expert in their field.

Gary Klein is a renowned and expert researcher on decision-making and cites the following aspects that experts have the ability to see which novices do not.[196]

1. Experts see patterns that novices do not detect.
2. Experts see anomalies—events that did not happen.
3. Experts see the big picture (situational awareness).
4. Experts create opportunities and improvisations.
5. Experts have the ability to predict future events using their previous experiences.
6. Experts see differences too small for novices to detect.
7. Experts know their own limitations.

With an understanding of the differences between the experienced and the novice, we can begin to design a plan to

---

* The ten-year milestone is derived by taking what researchers have determined as ten thousand hours of practicing a complex task to gain true expertise (Gladwell, *Outliers*, p. 40). Ten thousand hours is divided into practicing a task three hours a day every day for ten years.

overcome the shortfalls. Fortunately, understanding that it isn't a "matter of intelligence, but a matter of experience" means that we can systematically set about gaining the experience necessary.

One way you could do this is by choosing an area that you can easily visit repeatedly without raising unnecessary attention to your presence. Establish a baseline for that location using one of the approaches discussed in the preceding sections. If you dedicate time to going back to that same location, confirming your baseline and observing every single person that comes through that area, you will begin to build that database of experiences that is the key difference between experts and rookies. When you believe that you have reached a level of success in your predictions for people in that one area, where you are observing both the similarities as well as the subtle differences between every person that enters, and can effectively communicate those observations, move on to a new location and repeat the process. As you continue to do this at every location you commonly visit, you will also begin to make the practice of profiling a habit, requiring less mental attention from you to "remember to profile."

The deliberate approach to establishing baselines will help guide your efforts initially and ensure that you systematically cover the entire area. Initially, this approach may limit your ability to comprehend the bigger picture. However, over time, you will rely less on the methods and seamlessly blend the steps together into a smooth activity.

One of the major difficulties you will need to overcome as you train yourself as a profiler is the lack of feedback you will receive for your observations. Without that feedback loop for your judgments and conclusions, you will never be able to learn from your mistakes and become a better observer. We recommend that you do this in areas where you can contact people and easily talk to people to confirm or deny your observations. It is we why often use Starbucks and malls during our classes because they are places we can go today and observe with a relatively low level of risk. This process of contacting people will also require that you use some cunning to elicit the information that you are seeking without letting the person know you have been observing them, ultimately expanding all of the file folders necessary for an expert profiler.

The goal for this development is for you to increase not only the success rate for your predictions, but also the confidence you have in your ability to profile. However, we also want to ensure you are realistic in your abilities, understand your limitations, and don't become overconfident in your skills. In his book *The Invisible Gorilla*, Christopher Chabris talks about his research on chess players and their perception of their rating, which shows how they rank compared with the rest of the chess world. He found that 75 percent of chess tournament players believed they were better than their published rating.[197] To reduce the variables in the research, he checked back on the same players a year later to find that they maintained the same ranking. The ranking was accurate, but the perception of the skill possessed by the chess players was inflated. The reason I bring the research from *The Invisible Gorilla* up is because there will always be more research that you could conduct and there will always be more scenarios that you could use to develop your ability or different settings for you to apply this skill. Overconfidence will result in incorrect predictions because you failed to take into account all of the information present. Learning is impossible without humility. We encourage confidence, not cockiness.

Training Resources on the Web

In an attempt to further assist you on this journey, we have also created a website for you to continue your training and education. The goal of the site is to support this book. We provide articles on other aspects of profiling, different viewpoints on the topics in the course, a reading list with reviews of the books that we use to develop new instructors which are referenced throughout this book, and most importantly, a video training section.

The intent of the website is to provide a library of videos and other training for you to develop your file folders, with accompanying articles for you to expand your view of what profiling has to offer. Videos allow us to watch a specific incident as many times as necessary to learn how to analyze behavior and associate it with a threat while also providing feedback. When other venues are not available, this video training can be conducted from your home to build your profiling foundation.

From the website, you can easily find our contact information, and we encourage you to tell us your stories so that we can continue to provide relevant and effective training. Tell us what you want to learn more about, and tell us about better ways we can use and apply the information discussed here.

Visit www.cp-journal.com

A Final Letter

Dear Reader:

Our goal for this book was simple: to make Marines, soldiers, law enforcement officers, and anyone else who has dedicated their life to protecting our society more effective in hunting our enemies and increasing their ability to recognize threats. These areas will make Marines more survivable on patrol, both while deployed and at home. The information in this book has been previously inaccessible to most Marines. We hope we changed that.

Developing into a profiler will be a rollercoaster ride. It certainly has been for us. There will be times when you think that this is the most fascinating thing you have ever done in your life. There will be other times when the frustration will seem insurmountable and you will want to take a break from analyzing every gesture that you are observing. That is completely natural. There will be times when you believe that your observations are absolutely spot on, and you will feel extremely confident in what you identify. Other times you will question yourself and feel that you are no closer to understanding humans than you were before you started studying this field. This is also natural, and you will get past it. But you have to stick to it. We do not claim to be experts. We only claim that we are striving to become experts and are taking the same journey that we hope we have inspired you to take. It isn't a journey that any of us will ever complete. As soon as you believe that you are in expert in your field, you will no longer have the drive to keep learning. Humans are diverse, adapting and changing; there is always something to learn. The six domains of combat profiling and the content in this book should provide you with the foundation to grow in this pursuit. Good luck.

Never Forget. Never Quit. *Semper Fidelis*.

Patrick Van Horne/Jason A. Riley

ENDNOTES

PART 1: THE WAR LAB

1. Gordon, Mazzetti, & Shanker, 2006.

2 Tyson 2006.

3 Wilson 2005, 2.

4 USMC 2009, fwd.

5 USMC 2009, 1.

6 Vargas and Martin 2013.

7 Grossman and Christensen 2007, 43-44.

8 Klein 1999, 89.

9 Klein 1999, 4.

10 Turvey 2008, 43.

11 Turvey 2008, 80.

12 Turvey 2008, 81.

PART 2: EVERY WE GO, THERE WILL BE PEOPLE

13 Carter 2012.

14 Patton Jr. 1983, 408.

15 USMC 1997, 22.

16 USMC 1997, 82-83.

17 Gigerenzer 2006, 120.

18 Ambady 2010, 271.

19 Stillman, Maner, & Baumeister 2010, 298-303.

20 Albrechtsen, Meissner and Susa 2009, 1052-1055.

21 Pentland 2008, 99.

22 Carey 2009.

23 Bechara, Damasio and Damasio 2003, 366.

24 Myers 2010, 373.

25 Navarro 2008, 23.

26 Navarro 2008, 27.

27 Navarro 2008, 27.

28 MacDonald 2008, 136.

29 Dudley and Todd 2001, 195.

30 Dudley and Todd 2001, 213.

31 Kologie 2001.

32 *Officers who cracked missing girl case* 2009.

33 Brown 2004, 47.

34 Brown 2004, 47.

35 Ekman and Friesen 2003, 27.

36 Pentland 2008, x.

37 Song, et al. 2010, 1021.

38 *Human Behavior is 93 Percent Predictable* 2010.

39 Knapp and Hall 2010, 66.

40 Vrij, Porter and Granhag 2010, 29.

41 Ekman 2007, xviii.

42 Pentland 2008, 18.

43 González, Hidalgo and Barabási 2008, 781.

44 Wolchover 2011.

45 Medina 2010, 84-88

46 Pentland 2008, 15.

PART 3: DETAIL

47 Bernton, et al. 2002.

<u>Kinesics</u>

48 Navarro 2008, 10; Pease and Pease 2006, 23-24.

49 Navarro 2008, 26.

50 Pease and Pease 2006, 21.

51 Knapp and Hall 2010, 136.

52 Navarro 2008, 66.

53 Navarro 2008, 102, 124-125.

54 Navarro 2008, 120-121.

55 Navarro 2008, 125.

56 Navarro 2008, 116-117.

57 Pease and Pease 2006, 36.

58 Pease and Pease 2006, 38.

59 Navarro 2008, 147-148.

60 Knapp and Hall 2010, 418-419.

61 Knapp and Hall 2010, 273.

62 Navarro 2008, 82.

63 Navarro 2008, 95-97.

64 Navarro 2008, 125.

65 Pease and Pease 2006, 36.

66 Navarro 2008, 105-106.

67 Knapp and Hall 2010, 284.

68 Navarro 2008, 73-74.

69 Navarro 2008, 69.

70 Navarro 2008, 86-87.

71 Navarro 2008, 86-87.

72 Navarro 2008, 88.

73 Pease and Pease 2006, 100.

74 Pease and Pease 2006, 105-106.

75 Pentland 2008, 5.

76 Navarro 2008, 35-50.

77 Knapp and Hall 2010, 9, 283.

78 Navarro 2008, 73-74.

79 Navarro 2008, 69.

80 Navarro 2008, 86.

81 Navarro 2008, 101-102.

82 Navarro 2008, 89.

83 Navarro 2008, 105-106.

84 Navarro 2008, 60.

85 Navarro 2008, 89; Knapp and Hall 2010, 413.

86 Navarro 2008, 88-89; Knapp and Hall 2010, 413.

87 Knapp and Hall 2010, 295.

88 Knapp and Hall 2010, 413.

89 Navarro 2008, 59-60.

90 Navarro 2008, 60-61.

91 Navarro 2008, 86-87; Knapp and Hall 2010, 141.

92 Knapp and Hall 2010, 224.

93 Knapp and Hall 2010, 229.

Biometrics

94 Plutchik 1994, 136.

95 Ekman 2007, 19-20.

96 Malmo 1975, 96.

97 Malmo 1975, 96.

98 Ekman 2007, 110.

99 Izard 1978, 329-330.

100 Izard 1978, 333.

101 Ekman 2007, 114.

102 Izard 1978, 330.

103 Kreiberg 2010, 400.

104 Izard 1978, 330.

105 Ekman 2007, 125.

106 Izard 1978, 356.

107 Ekman 2007, 152.

108 Ekman 2007, 154.

109 Ekman 2007, 156.

110 Kreiberg 2010, 404; see also Levinson 1992, 25.

111 Izard 1978, 379.

112 Kreiberg 2010, 403; see also Aboyoun and Dabbs Jr. 2010, 498.

113 Kreiberg 2010, 403.

114 Levinson 1992, 25.

115 Plutchik 1994, 137.

116 Andreassi 2000, 219.

117 Hess 1975, 7-92.

118 Cannon 1915, 35-36.

119 Ekman 2007, 130.

120 Ekman 2009, 142.

121 Porter and ten Brinke 2008, 512.

122 Porter and ten Brinke 2008, 512; also Ekman 2007, 130.

123 Godnig 2003, 95-99.

124 Grossman and Christensen 2007, 46-48.

125 Frijda 1986, 131.

126 Frijda 1986, 130.

127 Frijda 1986, 131.

128 Harris 2001, 892-893.

129 Harris 2001, 893.

130 Frijda 1986, 133.

131 Frijda 1986, 140.

132 Frijda 1986, 146.

133 Grossman and Christensen 2007, 30-31.

134 Pentland 2008, 13.

Proxemics

135 Barrett, et al. 2005, 314.

136 Mehrabian 1971, 1.

137 Hall 1966, 116-119.

138 Lawson 2001, 184.

139 Knapp and Hall 2010, 141.

140 Hall 1966, 119-120.

141 Hall 1966, 121-125.

142 Barrett, et al. 2005, 313.

143 Mehrabian 1981, 13.

Geographics

144 Rossmo 2000, 2.

145 Rossmo 2000, 91.

146 Rossmo 2000, 91.

147 Knapp and Hall 2010, 136.

148 Rossmo 2000, 120.

149 Gellman and Ricks 2002; see also Cruickshank 2001.

150 Mazzetti, Cooper and Baker 2001; see also Schmidle 2001.

Iconography

151 Shoham 2010, 988.

152 Shoham 2010, 988.

153 Ley and Cybriwsky 1974, 496.

154 Ley and Cybriwsky 1974, 503-504.

155 Mackey 2009.

156 Abawi 2010.

157 Shoham 2010, 987.

158 Loranzo, et al. 2011, 511.

159 Shoham 2010, 987; also, Palermo 2011, 507.

160 Palermo 2011, 507.

161 Palermo 2011, 508.

162 Heywood, et al. 2012, 56.

163 Loranzo, et al. 2011, 510.

164 Shoham 2010, 987.

165 Szlemko, et al. 2008, 1678.

Atmospherics

166 Haley 1989, 88.

167 Olson 2006, 196.

168 Barsade 2002, 645.

169 Olson 2006, 196.

170 Barsade 2002, 645.

171 Barsade 2002, 647-648.

172 Olson 2006, 196.

173 De Becker and Marquart 2008, 8.

174 Artwohl 2002, 19-20.

175 Keizer, Lindenberg and Steg 2008, 1681-1685.

176 Saito 2007, 11.

PART 4: TAKING ACTION

177 BBC.com 2010.

178 Ekman 2009, 80.

179 Grossman 1996, 4.

180 Grossman 1996, 39.

PART 5: APPLICATIONS

181 ABC News 2014.

182 Klein 1999, 149.

183 Klein 1999, 148-149.

184 Knapp and Hall 2010, 245; see also, Yabar, et al. 2006, 97.

185 Yabar, et al. 2006, 98.

186 Yabar, et al. 2006, 99.

187 Van Horne 2012.

188 Roggio and Lundquist 2013.

189 Shanker 2012.

190 Rugala and Isaacs 2012, 12.

191 FBI 2012.

192 Rugala and Isaacs 2012, 13.

193 Romano, Levi-Minzi, Rugala, Van Hasselt 2001.

194 Romano, Levi-Minzi, Rugala, Van Hasselt 2001.

195 Gladwell 2008, 41.

196 Klein 1999, 157.

197 Chablis and Simons 2010, 84.

BIBLIOGRAPHY

Abawi, Atia. *Afghan Flag Raised Over War-Torn Taliban Stronghold*. February 25, 2010. http://articles.cnn.com/2010-02-25/world/afghanistan.offensive_1_taliban-stronghold-afghan-government-afghan-flag?_s=PM:WORLD (accessed January 23, 2012).

ABC News. *Tip from target worker helps cops find abducted child*. January 9, 2014. http://abcnews.go.com/blogs/headlines/2014/01/tip-from-target-worker-helps-cops-find-abducted-child/

Aboyoun, Celso M., and James M. Dabbs Jr. "Influence of Autonomic Signals on Perception of Emotions in Embodied Agents." *Applied Artificial Intelligence* 24 (2010): 494-509.

Albrechtsen, Justin S., Christian A. Meissner, and Kyle J. Susa. "Can Intuition Improve Deception Detection Performance." *Journal of Experimental Social Psychology* 45 (2009): 1052-1055.

Ambady, Nalini. "The Perils of Pondering: Intuition and Thin Slice Judgments." *Psychological Inquiry* 21 (2010): 271-278.

Ambady, Nalini, Brett Conner, and Mark Hallahan. "Accuracy Of Judgments of Sexual Orientation From Thin Slices of Behavior." *Journal of Personality and Social Pyschology* 77 (1999): 538-547.

Andreassi, J.L. "Pupillary Response and Behavior." *Psychophysiology: Human Behavior and Physiological Response* (Lawrence Erlbaum Assoc), 2000: 218-233.

Artwohl, Andy. "Perceptual and Memory Distortions During Officer Involved Shootings." *FBI Law Enforcement Bulletin*, October 2002: 18-24.

Barrett, H. Clark, Peter M. Todd, Geoffrey F. Miller, and Philip W. Blythe. "Accurate Judgments of Intentions from Motion Cues Alone: A Cross-Cultural Study." *Evolution and Human Behavior* 26 (2005): 313-331.

Barsade, Sigal G. "The Ripple Effect: Emotional Contagion and Its Influence on Group Behavior." *Adminstrative Science Quarterly* 47 (2002): 644-657.

BBC.com. *Mapping US Drone and Islamic Militant Attacks in Pakistan*. July 22, 2010. http://www.bbc.co.uk/news/world-south-asia-10733013.

Bechara, Antoine, Hanna Damasio, and Antonio R. Damasio. "Role of the Amygdala in Decision Making." *Annals of the New York Academy of Science*, 2003: 356-369.

Bernton, Hal, Mike Carter, David Heath, and James Neff. "The Terrorist Within—The Story Of One Man's Holy War Against America." *The Seatle Times*, June 23, 2002.

Brafman, Ori, and Rom Brafman. *Sway: The Irresistible Pull of Irrational Behavior*. New York, NY: Broadway Books, 2008.

Brown, Donald E. "Human Universals, Human Nature, Human Culture." *Daedalus*, Fall 2004: 47-54.

Cannon, Walter B. *Bodily Changes in Pain, Hunger, Fear, And Rage*. New York: D. Appleton and Company, 1915.

Carey, Benedict. *In Battle, Hunches Prove to Be Valuable*. July 29, 2009. http://www.nytimes.com/2009/07/28/health/research/28brain.html?_r=3&pagewanted=print.

Carlson, Neil R. *Physiology of Behavior, 9th Edition*. New York: Pearson, 2007.

Carrere, Sybil, and John Gottman. "Predicting Divorce Among Newlyweds From the First Three Minutes of a Marital Conflict Discussion." *Family Process* 38 (1999): 293-301.

Carter, Sara A. *Marine's career threatened by controversial rules of engagement*. March 19, 2012. http://washingtonexaminer.com/marines-career-threatened-by-controversial-rules-of-engagement/article/167369 (accessed March 19, 2012).

Chablis, Christopher, and Daniel Simons. *The Invisible Gorilla: How Our Intentions Deceive Us*. New York: Broadway Paperbacks, 2010.

Cruickshank, Paul. "Osama Bin Laden's Escape: A Tale of Subterfuge and Hard Cash." *cnn.com*, April 27, 2001.

De Becker, Gavin. *The Gift Of Fear: Survival Signals That Protect Us From Violence*. New York, NY: Dell Publishing, 1997.

De Becker, Gavin, and Jeff Marquart. *Just 2 Seconds*. Studio City, CA: Gavin de Becker Center for the Study And Reduction of Violence, 2008.

Dowling, John E. *Creating Mind: How the Brain Works*. New York: W. W. Norton & Company, 1998.

Dudley, Thomas, and Peter M. Todd. "Making Good Decisions with Minimal Information: Simultaneous and Sequential Choice." *Journal of Bioeconomics* 3 (2001): 195-215.

Ekman, Paul. *Emotions Revealed: Recognizing Faces and Feelings To Improve Communication and Emotional Life*. New York, NY: St. Martin's Press, 2007.

Ekman, Paul. *Telling Lies: Clues to Deceit in the Marketplace, Politics, and Marriage*. New York, NY: W. W. Norton & Company, 2009.

Ekman, Paul, and Wallace Friesen. *Unmasking the Face: A Guide To Recognizing Emotions from Facial Expressions*. I S H K, 2003.

FBI. *Crime in the United States*. 2012. http://www.fbi.gov/about-us/cjis/ucr/crime-in-the-u.s/2012/crime-in-the-u.s.-2012/violent-crime/violent-crime

Force Science Research Center. *Edged Weapon Defense: Is or Was the 21-foot Rule Valid?* 05 23, 2005. http://www.policeone.com/edged-weapons/articles/102828-Edged-Weapon-Defense-Is-or-was-the-21-foot-rule-valid-Part-1/ (accessed 01 10, 2012).

Frijda, Nico H. *The Emotions.* Cambridge: Cambridge University Press, 1986.

Gellman, Barton, and Thomas E. Ricks. "U.S. Concludes Bin Laden Escaped at Tora Bora Fight: Failure to Send Troops in Pursuit Termed Major Error." *Washington Post*, April 17, 2002: A01.

Gigerenzer, Gerd. "Bounded and Rational." In *Contemporary Debates in Cognitive Science*. Edited by R.J. Stainton. Oxford: Blackwell, 2006.

Gigerenzer, Gerd. *Gut Feelings: The Intelligence of the Unconscious.* New York: Penguin Books, 2007.

Gigerenzer, Gerd, and Stephani Kurzenhauser. "Fast and Frugal Heuristics In Medical Decision Making." *Science and Medecine in Dialogue*, 2005: 3-15.

Gladwell, Malcolm. *Outliers: The Story Of Success.* New York: Little, Brown and Company, 2008.

Gladwell, Malcolm. *The Tipping Point: How Little Things Can Make a Big Difference.* New York, NY: Back Bay Books / Little, Brown and Company, 2002.

Godnig, Edward C. "Tunnel Vision: Its Causes and Treatment Strategies." *Journal of Behavioral Optometry*, 2003: 95-99.

González, Marta C., César A Hidalgo, and Albert-László Barabási. "Understanding Human Mobility Patterns." *Nature*, 2008: 779-782.

Gordon, Michael R., Mark Mazzetti, and Thom Shanker. *Bombs Aimed At G.I.'s in Iraq Are Increasing.* August 17, 2006. http://www.nytimes.com/2006/08/17/world/middleeast/17military.html?_r=1&oref=slogin (accessed Januaray 11, 2012).

Grossman, Dave. *On Killing.* New York: Bay Back Books, 1996.

Grossman, Dave, and Loren W. Christensen. *On Combat: The Psychology and Physiology of Deadly Conflict in War and In Peace.* Chicago: Warrior Science Group, 2007.

Haley, Patrick. "Ambush At Union II." *Marine Corps Gazette*, November, 1989.

Hall, Edward T. *The Hidden Dimension.* New York: Anchor Books, 1966.

Harrington, Jinni A. "Proxemics, Kinesics, and Gaze." *The New Handbook of Methods in Nonverbal Behaviour Research.* Oxford: Oxford University Press, 2005: 137-138.

Harris, Christine. "Cardiovascular Responses of Embarrassment and Effects of Emotional Suppression in a Social Setting." *Journal of Personality and Social Psychology* 81 (2001): 886-897.

Hess, Eckhard H. *The Tell-Tale Eye: How Your Eyes Reveal Hidden Thoughts and Emotions.* New York: Van Hostrand Reinhold Company, 1975.

Heywood, Wendy, et al. "Who Gets Tattoos? Demographic and Behavioral Correlates of Ever Being Tattooed in a Representative Sample of Men and Women." *Annals of Epidemiology* 22 (2012): 51-56.

Hugdahl, Kenneth. *Psychophysiology: The Mind-Body Perspective*. Cambridge: Harvard University Press, 1995.

Human Behavior is 93 Percent Predictable, Research Shows. 2010. http://www.northeastern. edu/news/stories/2010/02/network_science.html.

Izard, Carroll E. *Human Emotions*. New York: Plenum Press, 1978.

Jinni A. Harrington, "Proxemics, Kinesics, and Gaze," pages 137-198 in *The New Handbook of Methods in Nonverbal Behaviour Research* [eds. Jinni A. Harrington, R. Rosenthal, and K. R. Scherer; Oxford: Oxford University Press, 2005].

Katlin, Edward S., Stefan Wiens, and Arne Ohman. "Nonconscious Fear Conditioning, Visceral Perception, and the Development of Gut Feelings." *Psychological Science* 12 (2001): 366-370.

Keizer, Kees, Siegwart Lindenberg, and Linda Steg. "The Spreading Of Disorder." *Science* 322 (2008): 1681-1685.

Klein, Gary. *Sources of Power: How People Make Decisions*. Cambridge, MA: The MIT Press, 1999.

Klein, Gary. *Streetlights and Shadows: Searching for the Keys to Adaptive Decision Making*. Cambridge, MA: The MIT Press, 2009.

Knapp, Mark L., and Judith A Hall. *Nonverbal Communication in Human Interaction, 7th Edition*. Boston, MA: Wadsworth, Cengage Learning, 2010.

Kologie, Carl. *Injury in Afghanistan can't keep this Marine down*. July 3, 2001. http://www. indianagazette.com/news/indiana-news/carl-kologie-injury-in-afghanistan-cant-keep-this-marine-down,105061/.

Kreiberg, Sylvia D. "Autonomic Nervous Systems Activity in Emotion: A Review." *Biological Psychology* 84 (2010): 394-421.

Krueger, Juliane. *Nonverbal Communication: Seminar Paper*. Norderstedt: Grin Verlag, 2005.

Kuntz, Albert. *The Autonomic Nervous System*. Philadelphia: Lea and Febiger, 1953.

Lawson, Bryan. *The Language Of Space*. Burlington, MA: Elsevier Ltd, 2001.

Levinson, Robert. "Autonomic Nervous System Differences Among Emotions." *Psychological Science* 3 (1992): 23-27.

Ley, David, and Roman Cybriwsky. "Urban Graffiti as Territorial Markers." *Annals of the Association of American Geographers* 64, no. 4 (Dec 1974): 491-505.

Loranzo, Alicia T. Rozychi, Robert D. Morgan, Danielle D. Murray, and Femina Varghese. "Prison Tattoos as a Reflection Of the Criminal LIfestyle." *International Journal of Offender Therapy and Comparative Criminology* 55 (2011): 509-529.

MacDonald, Matthew. *Your Brain The Missing Manual: How to Get the Most From Your Mind*. Sebastopol, CA: O'Reilly Media, 2008.

Mackey, Robert. *At War: Taliban Claim to Raise a Flag Over Nuristan*. October 7, 2009. http://atwar.blogs.nytimes.com/2009/10/07/taliban-claim-to-raise-a-flag-over-nuristan/ (accessed February 2, 2012).

Malmo, Robert B. *On Emotions, Needs, and Our Archaic Brain*. New York: Hold, Rinehart and Winston, Inc, 1975.

Mast, Marianne Schmid, and Judith A. Hall. "Who is the Boss And Who Is Not? Accuracy of Judging Status." *Journal of Nonverbal Behavior* 28 (2004): 145-163.

Mazzetti, Mark, Helene Cooper, and Peter Baker. "Behind The Hunt For Bin Laden." *New York Times*, May 2, 2001.

Medina, John. *Brain Rules: 12 Principles For Surviving and Thriving at Work, Home, and School*. Seattle, WA: Pear Press, 2010.

Mehrabian, Albert. *Silent Messages: Implicit Communication of Emotions and Attitudes*. Belmont, CA: Wadsorth, 1981.

Myers, David G. "Intuition: Its Powers And Perils." *Psychological Inquiry* 21 (2010): 371-377.

Navarro, Joe. *What Every Body Is Saying*. New York, NY: Harper Collins Publishers, 2008.

Officers who cracked missing girl case: Something wasn't right. August 21, 2009. http://www.cnn.com/2009/CRIME/08/31/missing.girl.officers/.

Olson, Kenneth R. "A Literature Review of Social Mood." *The Journal Of Behavioral Finance* 7 (2006): 193-203.

Palermo, George B. "The Skin And Freedom Of Speech." *International Journal of Offender Therapy and Comparative Criminology* 55 (2011): 507-508.

Patterson, Miles L. *Nonverbal Behavior: A Functional Perspective*. New York, NY: Springer-Verlag, 1983.

Patton Jr., George S. *War As I Knew It*. New York: Bantam, 1983.

Pease, Allan, and Barbara Pease. *The Definitive Guide Of Body Language*. New York, NY: Bantam Dell, 2006.

Pentland, Alex. *Honest Signals: How They Shape Our World*. Cambridge, MA: The MIT Press, 2008.

Plutchik, Robert. *The Psychology and Biology Of Emotion*. New York: Harper Collins, 1994.

Porter, Stephen, and Leanne ten Brinke. "Reading Between The Lies: Identifying Concealed and Falsified Emotions In Universal Facial Expressions." *Psychological Science* 19, no. 5 (2008): 508-514.

Roggio, Bill, and Lisa Lundquist. "Green-on-blue attacks in Afghanistan: the data." *The Long War Journal*, updated Oct. 26, 2013 (http://www.longwarjournal.org/archives/2012/08/green-on-blue_attack.php)

Romano, Stephen J, Micol E Levi-Minzi, Eugene A. Rugala, and Vincent B. Van Hasselt, "Workplace Violence Prevention: Readiness and Response," FBI (http://www.fbi.gov/stats-services/publications/law-enforcement-bulletin/january2011/workplace_violence_prevention

Rossmo, D. Kim. *Geographic Profiling*. New York: CRC Press, 2000.

Rugala, Eugene A, and Arnold R. Isaacs. *Workplace Violence: Issues in Response* (Critical Incident Response Group, FBI).

Saito, Mamiko. "Second-Generation Afghans In Neighboring Countries. From Mojaher to Hamwatan: Afghans Return Home." *Afghanistan Research and Evaluation Unit*, 2007: 11.

Schmidle, Nicholas. "Getting Bin Laden." *The New Yorker*, August 8, 2001.

Shanker, Thom. "General Notes Taliban Coercion in Some Attacks on Troops," *The New York Times*, Aug. 23, 2012 (http://www.nytimes.com/2012/08/24/world/asia/general-notes-taliban-coercion-in-some-attacks-on-troops-in-afghanistan.html?_r=2&ref=world&)

Shoham, Efrat. "Signs of Honor Among Russian Inmates In Israel's Prisons." *International Journal of Offender Therapy and Comparative Criminology* 54 (2010): 984-2003.

Song, Chaoming, Zehui Qu, Nicholas Blumm, and Albert-László Barabási. "Limits of Predictability in Human Mobility." *Science*, 2010: 1018-1021.

Stillman, Tyler F., Jon K. Maner, and Roy F. Baumeister. "A Thin Slice of Violence: Distinguishing Violent From Nonviolent Sex Offenders At A Glance." *Evolution and Human Behavior* 31 (2010): 298-303.

Szlemko, William J., Jacob A. Benfield, Paul A. Bell, Jerry L. Deffenbacher, and Lucy Troup. "Territorial Markings as a Predictor of Driver Aggression and Road Rage." *Journal of Applied Social Psychology* 38 (2008): 1664-1668.

Ten Brinke, L, and S. Porter. "Cry Me A River: Identifying The Behavioral Consequences of Extremely High-Stakes Interpersonal Deception." *Law and Human Behavior*, 2010: Online.

Tully, Elizabeth. *The Forebrain*. Philadelphia: Chelsea House Publishing, 2006.

Turvey, Brent E. *Criminal Profiling, Third Edition: An Introduction to Behavioral Evidence Analysis*. San Diego: Academic Press, 2008.

Tyson, Ann Scott. *U.S. Casualties in Iraq Rise Sharply*. October 8, 2006. http://www.washingtonpost.com/wp-dyn/content/article/2006/10/07/AR2006100700907.html (accessed 2012).

USMC. *Marine Corps Doctrinal Publication (MCDP) 5 - Planning*. Washington, DC: Department of the Navy, 1997.

USMC. *Marine Corps Interim Publication (MCIP) 3-11.01 - Combat Hunter*. Washington, DC: Department of the Navy, 2009.

Van Horne, Patrick. *Threats Inside The Wire: Preventing Green on Blue Attacks*. www.cp-journal.com/library. April 23, 2012.

Vargas, Ramon Antonio, and Naomi Martin. *NOPD radio traffic shows shot officer was not told gunman was still at Dollar General*. 2 26, 2013. http://www.nola.com/crime/index.ssf/2013/02/nopd_radio_traffic_shows_shot.html (accessed 2 26, 2013).

Vrij, Aldert, Stephen Porter, and Par Anders Granhag. "Pitfalls and Opportunities in Nonverbal and Verbal Lie Detection." *Psychological Science in the Public Interest*, 2010: 89-121.

Wilson, Clay. "Improvised Explosive Devises in Iraq." *Congressional Research Service Report For Congress*. November, 2005.

Wolchover, Natalie. *Science Shows You How to Win at 'Rock, Paper, Scissors'*. August 16, 2011. http://www.msnbc.msn.com/id/44162400/ns/technology_and_science-science/t/science-shows-you-how-win-rock-paper-scissors/#.T0iIrXlvfzs.

Yabar, Yahelia, Lucy Johnston, Lynden Miles, and Victoria Peace. "Implicit Behavioral Mimicry: Investigating the Impact Of Group Membership." *Journal Of Nonverbal Behavior* (Springer Science and Business Media Inc) 30 (July, 2006): 97-113.

About the Authors

Patrick Van Horne is the founder and CEO of *The CP Journal*, a behavioral analysis training company. His firm provides training support to the U.S. military, federal and local law enforcement agencies and the private security industry. Van Horne is a former infantry officer in the United States Marine Corps, earning the rank of Captain before returning to the private sector. His company's training programs are focused on teaching people how to prevent violent acts from occurring and finding attackers hiding in plain sight.

Jason A. Riley is currently a Major in the United States Marine Corps Reserve, with over six years on active duty. While with 1st Battalion, 2nd Marine Regiment, he served as an infantry platoon commander, company executive officer, and company commander, and deployed twice to Iraq with the 24th and 22nd Marine Expeditionary Units. He also served as a combat advisor to the Afghan National Army in an eastern province of Afghanistan. From 2009 until 2011, he was a mobile training team leader Officer-in-Charge with the Combat Hunter program at the School of Infantry (West). There, he developed training courses and taught behavioral profiling, among other duties. He currently serves with a reserve unit at Camp Pendleton, California. Jason is also pursuing his PhD.